CASPER MOUNTAIN

The Magic Yesterday and Today

BY

VAUGHN STEPHEN CRONIN

1998
Library of Congress Registration Number: TXU-843-862
Vaughn's Publishing

Printed by:  Endeavor Books-Mountain States Litho
133 S. McKinley
Casper, WY 82601
(307) 265-7410

Dedicated to
Those who love Nature
and
Casperites all over the world.
You know who you are.

CASPER MOUNTAIN

Photos taken the summer of 1996, by Vaughn S. Cronin.

TABLE OF CONTENTS

FOREWORD IX

MAPS

    U.S. GEOLOGICAL SURVEY MAP X

    HISTORICAL 1940 MAP XI

    QUICK SPOT GUIDE XIII

    TIME LINE XIV

GENERAL INFORMATION

    GENERAL INFORMATION 1

    TEN DO'S AND DON'TS 5

EAST END OF CASPER MOUNTAIN:

    HAT SIX 9

    FISH HATCHERY AND HAT SIX FALLS 11

    MYSTERY LUMBER CAMP 17

    BLACK CHOPPERS 19

    BROOKS 21

    CY RANCH 27

GARDEN CREEK ROAD:

    MAP AND QUICK SPOT GUIDE – GARDEN CREEK ROAD 30

    BLOODY TURNIP 31

    CAMP DODGE AND FORT CASPAR 33

    JOHNNY "HAPPY JACK" ALLEN 39

    FRED PATEE 43

    DEFY GRAVITY 49

    GARDEN CREEK FALLS 50

    BRIDLE TRAIL 55

TABLE OF CONTENTS

CASPER MOUNTAIN ROAD:

MAP AND QUICK SPOT GUIDE – CASPER MOUNTAIN ROAD	66
ELKHORN CANYON	69
HAIRPIN CURVES	73
LOOKOUT POINT	77
ROCK CLIMBING	82
SNOWSHOEING	85
ASBESTOS SPRING & ASBESTOS MINE	89
MOUNTAINEER'S MERCANTILE	99

ROAD TO HOGADON:

MAP AND QUICK SPOT GUIDE – ROAD TO HOGADON	105
STREET CAR	106
DAVY CROCKETT	107
CAMP SACAJAWEA	111
TOWER	113
ADAMS ARCHERY RANGE	114
COPPEROPOLIS	119
EADSVILLE	124
HOGADON SKI AREA	134

ROAD FROM JUNCTION TO MUDDY MOUNTAIN:

MAP AND QUICK SPOT GUIDE – JUNCTION TO MUDDY MOUNTAIN	144
OLD SKI AREAS	145
BRAILLE TRAIL	147
CROSS COUNTRY SKIING	148
THE CASPER MOUNTAIN LIONS CAMP	154
A NATURAL BRIDGE	156

TABLE OF CONTENTS

    BEAR TRAP MEADOW 158

    HIDDEN CAVERN 167

    TOWER HILL 169

    EAST END ROAD 171

    CRIMSON DAWN 173

    OUTER DRIVE ROAD 187

WEST END OF CASPER MOUNTAIN:

    MAP AND QUICK SPOT GUIDE – THE WEST END 194

    WOLF CREEK 195

    SQUAW CREEK 198

    RED BUTTE 204

    JACKSON CANYON 207

    FIRST CABIN IN WYOMING 213

    COAL MOUNTAIN ROAD 217

BIBLIOGRAPHY 219

INTERVIEWS 221

GLOSSARY OF TERMS 223

INDEX 227

PEOPLE INDEX 235

ACKNOWLEDGMENTS 241

ABOUT THE AUTHOR 242

CASPER MOUNTAIN

This photo competed at the Wyoming State Fair at Douglas, Wyoming in 1996.
Photo by Vaughn S. Cronin.

FOREWORD

Since I was a child, I have enjoyed looking at the mountain from town. Many feel that access to the mountain is limited by one main road, to the point that many locals and tourists alike feel that there is very little to do on the mountain. The Public Library had little information on the mountain that wasn't involved with geology, or Eadsville. Casper College had a good history on the mountain. Other sources of information included; the State Archives at Cheyenne, and the University of Wyoming. Good books on the mountain are rare. I started to hike areas and compile information. I also bought a camera and a computer. Past experience gave me quite a bit of knowledge about the mountain, being a Casper native, skiing both cross country and downhill on the mountain, although I learned much more by doing this project. Formatting a disk and starting writing. I created a table of contents that I used as my outline and guide, complete with maps, index, bibliography, glossary and acknowledgments so I could add to those areas as I went. Map mileage will vary from vehicle to vehicle. I used three vehicles and two books as sources of mileage.

Historical dates vary from book to book and brother to sister. For example, officials are elected in November and take office the following year, so there be a one year discrepancy. Even dates in the same book may conflict. Dates have varied as much as twenty years on topics like Mormon migration over the Oregon Trail. The Time-line in this book is as accurate as I could make it. I have had others review the book for accuracy, as well as using several written sources.

Interviews I had were extremely fascinating as I learned about the Littlefield family, Oly Fougstedt, Pistol Billy Mosteller, Davy Crockett and others, but the people giving the interviews were as interesting as the stories they told. Some of the land owners are reluctant to share their land, mostly out of fear of losing what they have. Vandalism, littering, arson and theft have soured many a landowner in the Casper Mountain area. Signs marking some of the points of interest that I will mention are rare. I hope that this book provides information that will stimulate interest in our natural resource, Casper Mountain. Enjoy!

VAUGHN STEPHEN CRONIN

CASPER MOUNTAIN AND AREA IN THE 1970'S

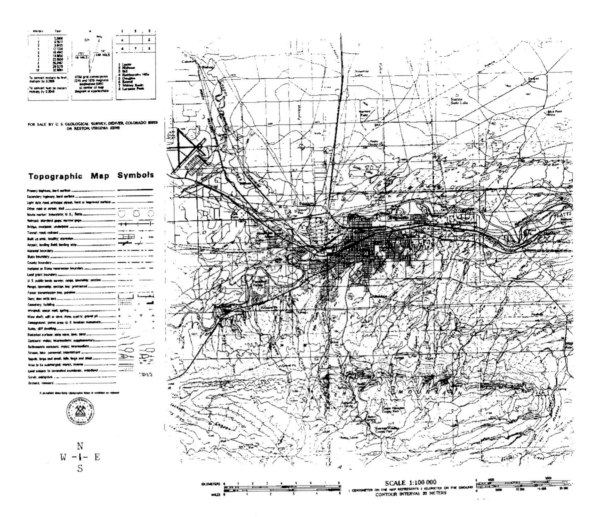

* This map is adapted from the U.S. Geological Survey

1940'S MAP OF THE CASPER AREA

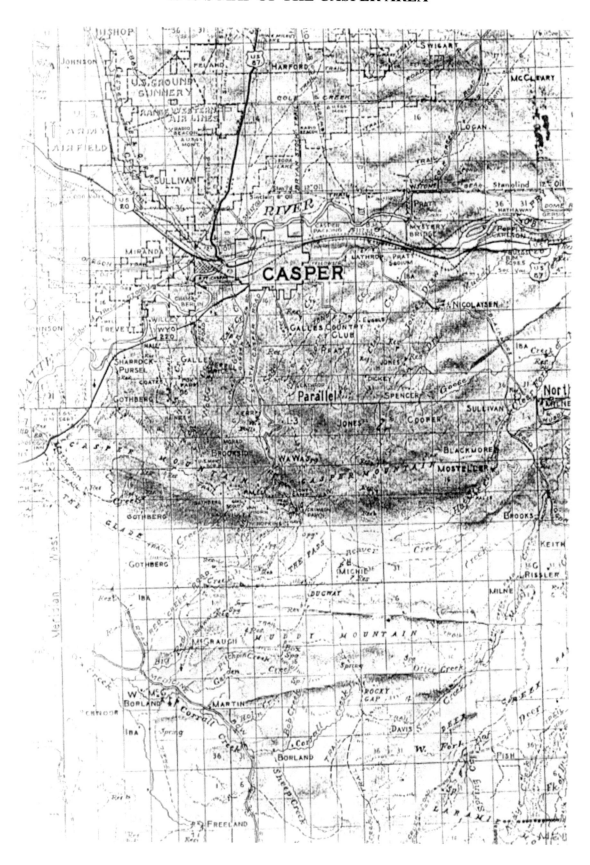

CASPER MOUNTAIN

Photos by Vaughn S. Cronin. Previous two pages – 1970's map versus a 1940's map.

QUICK SPOT GUIDE

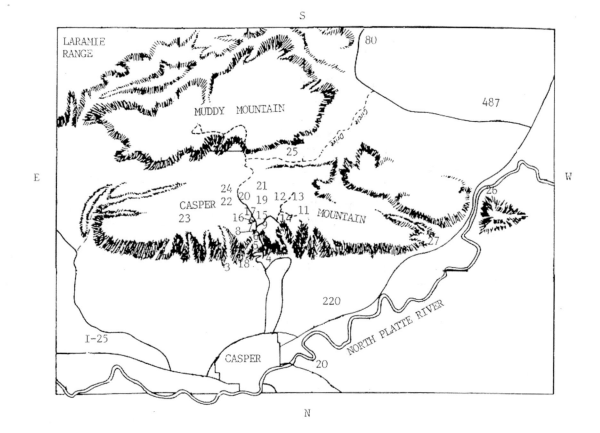

* Note that this map is "upside down" from a normal map.

1. Fish Hatchery
2. Sawmill
3. Elkhorn Canyon
4. Garden Creek Falls
5. Look Out Point
6. Rock Climbing Area
7. Asbestos Turn
8. Mountaineer's Mercantile
9. Streetcar
10. Camp Sacajawea
11. World War II Beacon
12. Archery Range
13. Eadsville
14. Hogadon
15. Nursery Ski Course Site
16. Braille Trail
17. Cross Country Ski Area
18. Window Rock
19. Lions Camp
20. Bear Trap Meadow
21. Casper Mountain Cave/Crystal Cave
22. Tower Hill
23. East End Road
24. Crimson Dawn
25. Outer Drive Road
26. First Cabin Site
27. Jackson Canyon
28. Goose Egg Ranch

TIME LINE

Middle Prehistoric Period circa 11,000 years ago or 9,000 B. C.
Paleo Indian Activity
~

1739 – North Platte River named
1805 – Sacajawea lead Lewis & Clark Expedition
1808 – First white man, John Colter, was in region
1812 – Astoria (Stuart) Cabin built
1830 – Upper crossing of the North Platte River (later Mormon Ferry)
1840 – Oregon Trail traveled; first activity at future Ft Caspar
1847 – Brigham Young lead Mormons across Wyoming; Mormon Ferry built
1852 – Reshaw Bridge Built; Mormon Ferry ceased operation
1858 – Garden Creek named; Guinard built bridge at what is now Fort Caspar
1859 – First permanent occupation at Fort Caspar site, or Platte Bridge Station
1860 – Cross Country Skiing came to Wyoming; Pony Express was started
1861 – B. B. Brooks born; Telegraph completed in WY, Vol. Cavalry at Platte Bridge Station
1862 – Casper Mountain was known as "Black Hills"
1865 – Camp Dodge built and Indian battle of Camp Dodge ensues; Reshaw Bridge abandoned/burned; LT Caspar Collins killed at Battle of Platte Bridge; SGT Amos Custard killed at Battle of Red Buttes; Fort Caspar named; Casper Mountain named; James M. Ashley introduced bill to make Wyoming a Territory
1867 – Fort Caspar abandoned; wood from fort and bridge were reused at Fort Fetterman or burned by Indians; Wyoming became a territory
1869 – Oregon Trail abandoned because of Transcontinental Railroad
1870 – Wyoming is first state granting women voting rights; Esther Hobart Morris first female Justice of the Peace in the U.S.
1871 – Hayden Expedition crossed Wyoming
1873 – Ranching started in Wyoming
1876 – CY Ranch started
1877 – Goose Egg Ranch started
1880 – Eadsville and mining began on mountain; Asbestos Road/Hogadone Trail built
1882 – V-V Ranch began operation
1884 – Wyoming Cattle depression; sheep introduced to state
1886 – Severe Winter of '86-'87
1887 – First sheep wagon built in Rawlins, Wyoming
1888 – "Old Casper" built and named; railroad came to Casper
1890 – Wyoming 44th state granted statehood; Natrona County formed by splitting Carbon County 1/2 with Casper as County Seat; asbestos discovered by J.C. Hogadone
1891 – S. A. (Jack) Currier silver strike
1893 – First courthouse built on west side of David between Yellowstone & Midwest Ave
1894 – Earthquake; Carey Act
1895 – Flash flood at Garden Creek Falls killed four people; Casper's first courthouse built
1897 – Earthquake; Dr. J.F. Leeper reopened Galena Queen Mine
1902 – Telephone established
1905 – Bryant B. Brooks took office as Governor
1907 – Abby Brooks christened schooner "The Governor Brooks"
1908 – Casper's second Courthouse built; Eads horse theft charge
1910 – Joseph M. Carey elected Governor; Patee Road built

TIME LINE

1911 – Fredericks' Cabin built
1913 – Car licensing started
1914 – Bryant B. Brooks first president of Wyoming National Bank
1919 – Dusty Miller and Marshall Buxton drown in lake near B.B. Brooks ranch; Dr. Leeper died in Chicago
1920 – Freeland Post Office built; "Wyoming" Depression began; Brookside built
1922 – Earthquake; Girl Scouts were organized in Casper; Casper City Council obtained Fort Caspar land
1924 – J.M. Carey died
1925 – First Woman Governor in U.S.: Nellie Tayleo Ross, from Wyoming
1930 – Allen Cabin burned in the 30's
1931 – Mosteller Fish Hatchery built
1933 – CCC established; Bridle Trail Built
1936 – Ft Caspar restored
1937 – Wa-Wa Lodge going strong; Davy Crockett (grandnephew of famous Davy Crockett) died
1939 – "Wyoming" depression ended
1940 – Ski trails appeared; Streetcar located on mountain; second courthouse razed, third built.
1941 – Pearl Harbor
1942 – Jim Forsling died in winter storm
1946 – Bryant B. Brooks died
1949 – Severe winter
1952 – Mosteller Fish Hatchery ceased operation
1953 – Founder of Girl Scouts in England visited Casper
195? – Brookside Inn burned
1958 – Hogadon Ski Area began operation
1960 – Hogadon Ski Area acquired stockholders
196? – Earthquake; Bomb Shelters were being built in basements
1962 – Casper Mountain Road completed
196? – Asbestos Spring shut down
1969 – "Hellfighters" filmed near Casper
1970 – Bloody Turnip named (formerly called CY or Allen Canyon)
1972 – Elkhorn Hermit
1973 – Neal Forsling donated Crimson Dawn to Parks Department
1975 – Braille Trail completed
1976 – Steve Lund made archaeological record of Casper Mountain; second structure at Nursery Ski Course burned
1978 – Fire on face of mountain
1985 – Fire
1986 – Earthquake
1994 – Fire at Elkhorn Canyon; Lights added for night skiing at Nordic Ski Area
1995 – 250,000 trees broken by heavy snow and wind
1996 – Black choppers reported doing military maneuvers; "Starship Troopers" filmed at Hell's Half Acre; Earthquake; Climbing death at Garden Creek Falls
1997 – Earthquake

Historians disagree on some of these dates

CASPER MOUNTAIN

Fire in 1994 on the north face of Casper Mountain. Photos from the Moore Collection.

CASPER MOUNTAIN

"Ghost Town" fire fighting trucks at Bear Trap Meadow, July 1996. Photos by Vaughn S. Cronin.

Left to right: Phil Santistevan, Chris Icenogle, and Pat Harshman stand ready at Bear Trap Meadow during the Summer Festival, 1996.

CASPER MOUNTAIN

Casper Mountain has a volunteer fire department, also known as the "Ghost Town Firefighters." Thanks to them, many potentially catastrophic fires have been minimized. Photos by Vaughn S. Cronin.

GENERAL INFORMATION

Casper Mountain is 1.8 miles south of Casper, Wyoming, which is the county seat for Natrona County, and the second largest city in Wyoming. The mountain has a year round population of about 150 residents. The mountain is located at the northern tip of the Laramie Mountain Range. Casper Mountain rises to an altitude of 8,130 feet (Casper is at an elevation of 5,123). The mountain is approximately three miles wide and ten miles long, running generally east-west.

"Casper Mountain is bounded to the southeast by Muddy Mountain (8,000 feet), and on the southwest by Coal Mountain (7,000 feet), "A FIELD GUIDE TO THE CASPER MOUNTAIN AREA," The Wyoming Field Science Foundation, 1978. A strip of land approximately 1/4 mile wide separates the three mountains. Casper Mountain has a fault, or break in the rocks, running east-west, along its north side. Its path is at about the lower tree line. This general structure of the mountain is a faulted anticline. An anticline is an up fold of the rocks. Rocks on the south side (backside) are generally inclined upwards in a much more gentle slope. Much of the mountain is inaccessible, with a steep grade in excess of 25% slope, on the north face of the mountain.

Earthquakes have struck the mountain area in written memory. In 1894 it was reported that dishes crashed to the floor and people were thrown from their beds. At first light residents were coming down the mountain as fast as possible. Other tremors occurred in 1897, and 1922. In the 1960's structural damage was done to property in the Garden Creek Drainage including the Shady-nook cabin. In 1986 and 1996, other slight tremors occurred.

Steve Lund made an archaeological survey of Casper Mountain and the adjoining areas from 1972 until 1976. He made two reports one called THE ARCHAEOLOGICAL RECORD OF CASPER MOUNTAIN, 1976, and RECORDS IN STONE AND BONE, 1975. Several archaeological finds were made on the west end of the mountain and on top of the mountain. In his report, THE ARCHAEOLOGICAL RECORD OF CASPER MOUNTAIN, 1976 Steve Lund states, "The oldest projectile point known to have been found on the mountain was a Clovis point, which indicates inhabitation of the area for 11,000 years. However, very few Paleo-Indian points have been found on the mountain."

Animals such as mountain lions, bobcats, wolves, coyotes, elk, fox, turkey, sage grouse and bear were present in large numbers in the 1890's. Today most of those animals have been destroyed or crowded out. Luckily the deer population still remains strong on the mountain.

CASPER MOUNTAIN

Severe weather sometimes plagues the state. Bad winters include the winter of 1886-87, when the railroad and all of the highways were closed for months. Deep drifts and cold temperatures killed people, livestock and wild game. The winter of 1949 still holds many records for the coldest temperature set in the state. Nine million head of livestock died that winter. In KATHLEEN'S BOOK by Kathleen Hemry, she speaks of the United States Air Force having to fly feed in to the livestock and making hay drops in 1949. Kathleen's car was buried in snow. "It [the car] remained for weeks as the blizzard raged on and on." Chinook winds helped bring an end to the winter of 1949.

Chinook winds, although strong, bring warm moist air from the southwest that melt the frozen earth, so that wild game and livestock can graze. Ranchers welcome the Chinook winds.

Above, a picture of a plane used in 1949 to carry hay to cattle stranded and in need. Tim Mahoney and Joe Cronin were among those who guided pilots to ranches. Story has it that one of the men throwing bails of hay out of the plane fell out and walked to the next ranch. Photo by Ken Ball; courtesy of the Ken Ball family.

GENERAL INFORMATION

The winter of '49 dropped heavy snow on Casper Mountain. Each storm dropped several feet of snow, followed by another storm.

Photo courtesy of the Ken Ball family.

Lack of moisture cause fire danger in the summer. Casper Mountain has its own Volunteer Firefighters made up of Doctors, Judges and Ski Patrol Members. The mountain had severe fires in the 1870's. The mountain has a 100 year cycle for serious forest fires which is past due. In 1985 fire struck Casper Mountain. Residents were prohibited from starting fires for any purpose. Photo by McClure; Courtesy of Casper Star-Tribune.

CASPER MOUNTAIN

The photo below came from the Denver Post in January 1949. The Cronin family was housed in the Bureau Reclamation Housing in what is now Mills, Wyoming. The occupants had to use the back door from January 2, 1949 until early April. The wind piled a layer of dirt in between each layer of snow. The street in front of the house was also impassable. The drift went well into the vacant lot across the street. "Winds reaching 80 miles an hour slammed snow across the prairies like a barrage of shotgun pellets with temperatures as low as fifty below," Ed Bille WYOMING, A PICTORIAL OVERVIEW, Mountain States Lithographing, 1989.

TEN DO'S AND DON'TS

1. In the summer, don't take your pop into the outhouse with you, unless you like to share with flies.

2. Make sure all of the buttons on your 501 Jeans are fastened BEFORE you meet new people in the woods.

3. Believe all of the stories you hear about yellow snow.

4. Winter tip, don't get off of your skis on a new trail if the snow is six feet deep.

5. Believe all of the stories you hear about wind direction.

6. Don't wear your shorts on a long hike through the thistle bushes.

7. Don't fall asleep while sunbathing.

8. Make sure there is toilet paper in the outhouse BEFORE it's too late!

9. Put all of your food away before you go to sleep for the evening at your campsite, unless you want to meet wild animals.

10. Make sure you have your keys BEFORE you lock the door to your vehicle.

CASPER MOUNTAIN

EAST END

CASPER MOUNTAIN

Photo by Vaughn S. Cronin.

HAT SIX

Two miles east of Casper, off of Interstate 25, is the Brooks Hat Six Road. Older maps also refer to it as the Blackmore Road. Named after a brand, the Hat Six Ranch is north of the Brooks Ranch.

Photo by Dana Van Burgh with pilots Judy Logue and Linda Wackwitz; courtesy of the Wyoming Field Foundation.

Above is an aerial photo looking south, of the east end of Casper Mountain (right foreground). Deer Creek Park is in the distance (top left). Smith Creek, and Beaver Creek are in the foreground. The Clear Fork of Muddy Creek also flows north in the foreground. Hat Six Road crosses the lower left portion of the picture. Between Hat Six Hogback and the West Fork of Muddy Creek, on the east end of Casper Mountain, lies the site of the old fish hatchery. Some distance away are the Hat Six Falls.

CASPER MOUNTAIN

Below, Casper Mountain was the site of this 1882 roundup camp. Fort Caspar had been partially burned by Indians, who now were adjusting to the reservations. Rufus Rhoads was the foreman of this crew. The roundups brought cowhands from various outfits together. The main ranches of the day were the CY, V-V, and the Goose Egg. Photo courtesy of the Natrona County Pioneer Museum.

FISH HATCHERY AND FALLS

If you take Hat Six Road, you will see a 'dinosaur' like hogback, just off of the East End of Casper Mountain, known as the Hat Six Hogback. If you then follow the road between the hog back and the mountain to the end of the road, then follow the West Fork of Muddy Creek upstream, you will find the old fish hatchery. It is on private property and you should call the Mosteller ranch for permission to visit.

Charlie Mosteller remembers building the hatchery with his father William Mosteller (known as Pistol Billy), in 1931. They used dynamite and sledge hammers to make the raceways for the fish. The hatchery ceased operation in 1952.

Pistol Billy got his nickname two ways; first, he was told he had a big gun for being such a little guy, second, one day he was asked how close he could come to hitting an antelope without actually hurting the animal. Let's just say he got very close!

Some distance away you will find a beautiful falls. These falls are known as the Hat Six Falls. This is on private property and the public is restricted; I was not permitted to photograph the area. No wonder these falls are seen by so few. Eleanor Carrigen, Neal Forsling, Neal's two daughters and a man identified only as "some jerk" were lost for three days trying to get to the falls from Crimson Dawn by taking the wrong canyon.

Below is a picture of the old fish hatchery.

The water wheel was used to grind fish food. Scrap from a local packing house was used. Photos by Vaughn S. Cronin.

CASPER MOUNTAIN

These raceways were once used by fish at the old fish hatchery.

Charlie Mosteller and his wife once lived in this house at the hatchery. Photos by Vaughn S. Cronin.

FISH HATCHERY AND FALLS

"Pistol Billy" Mosteller homesteaded this area in 1884. Most of the original homestead is still under family control. Pistol Billy was noted for being ahead of his time as an innovator in food production. In what was once known as Crystal Canyon Garden, he built greenhouses to grow food for the miners at Eadsville, and to sell to the local restaurants in town. Billy sold fish from the hatchery, had an apple orchard, and produced honey.

Mining was also important in the Mosteller history. Claims named Tillie Miller and Klondyke, on the north side of the mountain between Hat Six and Goose Creeks, existed in 1897. Mr. A. E. Minium and Billy Mosteller had adjoining claims in the Goose Creek Canyon. F.W. Okie and Billy Mosteller were partners in their gold mines. Access to this area on the old jeep trail has been denied to the public by neighboring property owners.

Children went through middle school at an educational institution located on the Hat Six Road. The school is a now missing landmark. Ranchers from a large area brought their children there for school.

In more recent times the Mosteller Ranch has been host to motor cycle races, outdoor concerts, scouts, muzzle loading clubs, and a variety of other civic activities.

Right – Barrels once used inside the hatchery for fish food. Photo by Vaughn S. Cronin.

CASPER MOUNTAIN

Built in the early 1900's, these greenhouses provided food during the harsh winter months. Above – Water was diverted from the stream to run the water wheel in the greenhouse for electricity. The water was then used to water plants. Electricity was used for band saws in the machine shop, for bee supplies, and for other projects. Steam was used for heat. In 1924 or 1925, the original house and greenhouses all burned to the ground. Photos courtesy the Mosteller Collection.

FISH HATCHERY AND FALLS

Below – "Pistol Billy" Mosteller had a honey display at the State Exposition in Douglas, on an annual basis. This photo was taken in 1933; courtesy the Mosteller Collection.

Right – Jim Cridor and Charlie Mosteller work at Charlie's sawmill in the late 1940's. Photo courtesy the Mosteller Collection.

CASPER MOUNTAIN

Above – "Sawmill Miller's" sawmill in "The Big Canyon." Below – Drum wired to a tree nearby, and part of the mandrel. If you find this, leave it for the next person to see. Photos by Darin Walker.

MYSTERY LUMBER CAMP

In the book CASPER CHRONICLES, published by the Zonta Club, 1964, there is an account by Maude Garton of their home life after the 1895 flood at Garden Creek Falls. "After this, [the flood] father worked at a sawmill up in the Glades for three years. Mother taught school at the new sawmill for three or four years without pay as there was a need for a teacher for the numerous children of the camp including her own."

Several people have found an old abandoned lumber mill on the east end of Casper Mountain. When they go back to photograph it or show their friends they can't find it. The first houses that were built in "Old Casper" in 1888 got their lumber from the lumber mill on Casper Mountain. Is this the same lumber mill? In B.B. Brooks book, THE MEMOIRS OF BRYANT B. BROOKS, 1939, he says that they got the lumber for the first buildings in Casper at the sawmill "a few miles away" from his V-V ranch.

Three sawmills existed on Casper Mountain. The sawmill on the east end of the mountain is on the Clearfork of Muddy Creek. It was known as the Hahn Mill. The trail to this sawmill is overgrown. A capped spring is nearby, and a cabin still stands as well as the mandrel for the saw that once was powered by a steam engine. Another sawmill is one-half mile upstream from the Hahn Mill. This second sawmill was known as the Miller Sawmill. It was located by the Michie Cow Camp. The third sawmill, located in the Glades, was down Micro Road in Gothberg Draw, on the southwest portion of the mountain, west of Red Creek. The owner of that mill, Mr. Briden, cut himself in half. He had a habit of leaning with one hand against a pole. He made a mistake, cut his arm off and grabbed for the pole with the now missing arm, falling into the saw. His wife got the dogs into the house and went straight to town to get the coroner.

You are on private property if you see any of these sawmills. Don't go on these properties without permission.

This old sawmill shack can be seen on the north side of the canyon on the Clear Fork of Muddy Creek. The mandrel is in the grass about fifty yards up the drainage. This building had two rooms with a stove. This site is near the old Michie Cow Camp. Photo courtesy Dave Ball.

CASPER MOUNTAIN

This tree stump was a victim of progress in the early days. Photo by Darin Walker.

BLACK CHOPPERS

A bizarre story that has recently emerged is the tale of the black helicopters flying around Casper Mountain. Dave Zerbe, a local businessman, has brought the news to the media that black choppers have been on maneuvers for several months. Soldiers in black uniforms have been reported rappelling from the choppers, and Zerbe reportedly has shell casings from spent ammunition. Zerbe got involved when two black helicopters flew over his property and hovered just a few feet above the roof of his home. The horses in the corral became so frightened that they broke through the fence. The choppers were unmarked, so the search began for the owners and why were they hovering so low over his property. The search has taken him to a very sinister world.

Until the media got involved, the faithful would line up along Hat Six Road Wednesday through Friday, between 7:30 and 9:30 p.m., and watch for the phenomenon. The media dismissed the story as fiction. Ray Erbert from KVOC Radio "saw something out there;" to be more specific, lights from some type of flying aircraft. Ray told the author that the airport confirms something is being picked up by their radar. People who watched nightly had seen as many as twenty to seventy lights at once, and saw them land on Muddy Mountain, as well as "on the flat."

On the Internet http://freeamerica.com/gvcon2.html several articles by Harry V. Martin about black choppers in the Napa Valley in California exist that sound similar to the local phenomenon that Dave Zerbe and friends have witnessed and reported. Both have black, unmarked helicopters, "The occupants have been described as men wearing black uniforms carrying automatic weapons," BLACK HELICOPTERS, THEY DO EXIST, DESPITE LOCAL MEDIA SCORN, http://freeamerica.com/gvcon2.html, Harry V. Martin.

Sightings have also been made in: Massachusetts; Paris, Texas; Loring, Maine; Wurtsmith, Michigan; Malmstrom, Montana; New Mexico; Nebraska; Oklahoma; Kansas; Illinois; Arkansas; Wisconsin; Arizona; Minnesota; and Colorado. Media like the Los Angeles Times, and Denver Post have covered these stories.

Harry V. Martin's series says that these sightings can be linked to the Federal Emergency Management Agency (FEMA) in conjunction with the Sixth Army. The helicopters are able to decode numerous signals from various satellites using special technology and language. In this way they can intercept and compile messages from different countries using unlike systems.

Executive Order Number 12148 "authorizing the Federal Emergency Management Agency to take over the executive functions of government." BLACK HELICOPTERS OVER AMERICA, STRIKEFORCE FOR THE NEW WORLD ORDER, Jim Keith, IllumiNet Press, 1994. With the stroke of a pen the president can suspend the Constitution and the Bill of Rights in time of emergency. The government could then seize weapons, put people in "work camps," seize private property and a host of other things. FEMA was standing ready after the "Rodney King" verdict. If rioting would have erupted in several cities instead of just Los Angeles, FEMA would have stepped in to stop the calamity according to Jim Keith.

CASPER MOUNTAIN

The <u>Rock Springs Daily Rocket Miner</u> had a story in their August 14, 1996 edition entitled "Damaged Army Chopper Lands." The story ran 10 days after the incident. The spokesman was Col. Pierce from Ft. Bragg, North Carolina. The chopper from Ft. Campbell, Kentucky was attempting a mid-air refueling near Rawlins, Wyoming, when the refueling arm from a second aircraft struck the forward rotor of the helicopter. Different people will have varied views on this story; few, if any of the local ranchers say they have seen any choppers. Are several people from around they country fabricating the same fiction, or is there more going on than the average American is aware?

BROOKS

Bryant B. Brooks "bought" a trapper's cabin on his twenty-first birthday for six #4 traps and a sack of flour. Nestled among the willow bushes on Muddy Creek, and just six miles from Deer Creek, between Casper and Muddy Mountain, it became one of Wyoming's great ranches, running both sheep and cattle. B.B. Brooks had the ranch known as the V Bar V Ranch until his death in 1946. His wife ran the ranch until 1948, when it was sold to "Doc" Stuckenhoff. He ran the ranch located on Hat Six Road until shortly before his recent death.

B.B. Brooks born February 8, 1861, took office as Governor of Wyoming in 1905. Brooks and his family were the first to occupy the Governor's Mansion in Cheyenne after it was built. B.B. Brooks who was in his political life, active in decision making for the state on a number of issues including; the naming of Natrona County, mining, the railroad, ranching, and the oil industry. Brooks also had a schooner, "Governor Brooks," christened in his name, by his daughter, Abby, in 1907, and was the first president of the Wyoming National Bank of Casper in 1914.

Bryant B. Brooks also has two lakes in the state known as Brooks Lake. One of the lakes is north of Dubois that Brooks discovered in 1889 as well as Brooks Lake creek. The second lake is eighteen miles east of Casper on the site of the V-V ranch. It is said to be haunted in Mokler's HISTORY OF NATRONA COUNTY, as well as THE MEMOIRS OF B.B. BROOKS. Indian apparitions have been seen on the lake, and people as well as animals have disappeared or drowned on the lake.

Photo of B.B. Brooks in 1879 courtesy of Mary H. Nicolaysen and family.

CASPER MOUNTAIN

Below is a photo of the Brooks Ranch in the late 1800's. The house in the left foreground was the homestead house in which all of the children were born. This is the ranch where Jack "Post Hole" McGrath worked. B.B. Brooks was going to be gone for a month. He told Jack. McGrath to dig some post holes for a fence they wanted to build. When Brooks returned from his journey, "Naturally I wondered what my first hired hand had been doing while I was away. When I reached the cabin I found out. The line of post holes that he had going north during my absence was about the most discouraging thing I ever looked at, and to this day I have been trying to catch up with them." Later in THE MEMOIRS OF BRYANT B. BROOKS, The Arthur Clark Company, 1939 Brooks says, "Jack's great line of post holes was one of the seven wonders of the territory. He became renowned as Post Hole Jack." Photo courtesy Shelly Trumbull.

BROOKS

Right – Circa 1908 photo of B.B. Brooks courtesy of Shelly Trumbull.

Top of page 25 – A photo of the "new house" built in 1898. It had a large steam water tank inside of the house. After "Doc" Stuckenhoff bought the ranch, this house was condemned and razed because of the water tank in the attic. Bottom – B.B. Brooks in front of the Governor's Mansion in Cheyenne. B.B. Brooks was the first governor to occupy the mansion. Page 26 – The schooner "The Governor Brooks" christened by his daughter Abby and launched at Bath Maine in 1907. Bottom – Brooks Lake discovered in 1889 by B.B. Brooks north of Dubois.

CASPER MOUNTAIN

Below – The Brooks mansion built in Casper in 1924.

In 1910 Governor Brooks convened the Wyoming Oil Men's Convention. This later became known as The Rocky Mountain Gas and Oil Association. Below is a 1912 photo of one of the conventions. Oil has played a big part in our local economy during peacetime and for our defense during war. From the Patton Collection; courtesy of the Natrona County Pioneer Association.

BROOKS

CASPER MOUNTAIN

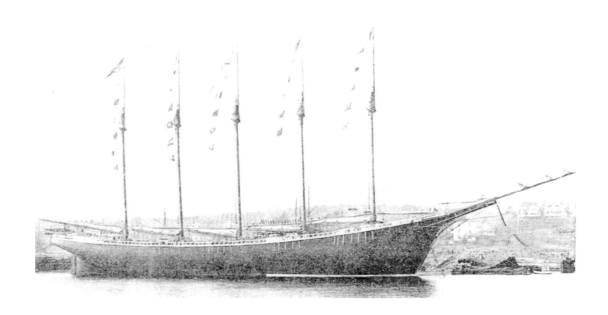

CY RANCH

It is hard to talk about the mountain without mentioning some of the things happening down on the flat land in Casper, and the CY Ranch started by Joseph M. Carey. The name CY, came from the first and last letters of the Carey name. J.M. Carey & Brother, who owned most of the land on which Casper is located, gave land to the railroad in an effort to get the line to run through Casper. Carey and the railroad then owned alternate lots, which Carey offered at low price for private sale. Cinders were common in people's eyes from the coal burning engines that pulled the train down the track. Fires along the route were also common.

CY Avenue was once the road to the CY Ranch House, once located east of Garden Creek, at the Fort Caspar Subdivision. This was the same path cowboys would follow home after a big night "on the town". The CY Ranch gave way to the Westridge subdivision and thus ended an era. Carey also owned the Goose Egg Ranch which he purchased in 1886.

Carey had an active career. As a Republican, Carey spoke out against prohibition in 1914. In 1917 he was forced to reverse his opinion. He served as U.S. Attorney for Wyoming Territory from 1869-71, Assistant Justice of the Wyoming Territorial Supreme Court 1872-76, and Territorial Delegate to Congress from 1885-1915. In 1889 Joseph M. Carey introduced the Wyoming Statehood Bill, eight months later in 1890, Wyoming became a state.

In 1894 the "Carey Act" was enacted to encourage the construction of reservoirs and irrigation systems, in an effort to help small farmers, on arid land. Carey was known as the "Father" of Wheatland Colony, using water from the Laramie River to irrigate 50,000 acres.

Carey was also the president of the Wyoming Stock Growers Association, a Mason, U.S. Senator, and Governor of the State of Wyoming from 1911-14. Carey died February 5, 1924.

CY Canyon is mentioned frequently in old accounts of the mountain, although you will have a tough time finding it on any present day map. Accounts of the Hogadone Trail, and flash floods at Garden Creek Falls, mention the canyon.

CASPER MOUNTAIN

GARDEN CREEK ROAD

MAP OF GARDEN CREEK ROAD ROUTE

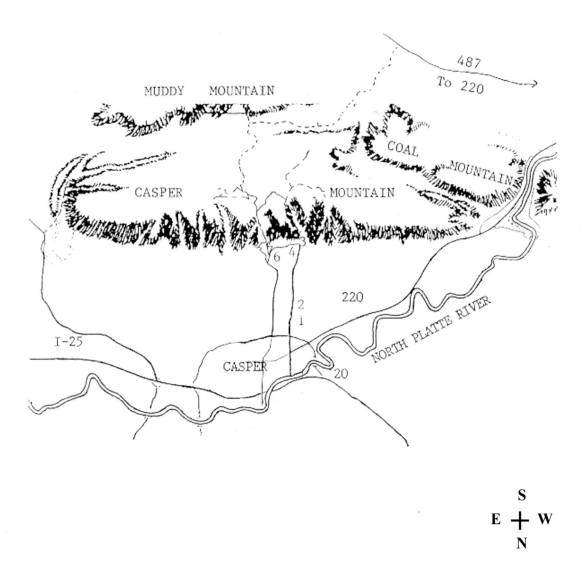

* Note that this is another upside down map. This is the way you would be oriented from Casper.

Places of Interest:

Starting at Wyoming Blvd. and S. Poplar, travel south on Poplar Street (Wyoming 252).

1. Mansion with Elevator	0.9 mi.	5. Hogadone Trail	3.9 mi.
2. Garden Creek Road	1.1 mi.	6. Gravity Hill	4.0 mi.
3. Bloody Turnip	2.6 mi.	7. Garden Creek Falls	4.0 mi.
4. Deer Feeder	3.2 mi.	8. End of Loop	4.3 mi.

BLOODY TURNIP

Starting at Wyoming Boulevard (Wyoming 258), and S. Poplar (Wyoming 252), travel south on Poplar Street. As you travel south you will notice some very expensive mansions along the route. One mansion in particular, on the right (west) side of the road has an elevator inside of the house.

As the road traverses to the right and starts its ascent by the old barn, the road changes its name to Garden Creek Road. Notice Garden Creek on your left as you climb the hill. When the road veers left (east) you are at Bloody Turnip. The Bloody Turnip area is located just south of the west end of the loop, at the bottom of Casper Mountain. When I was younger I would ride my bike to the Whitaker cabin. The hillside was covered with flowers. Before Whitaker purchased the, John D. Allen land, "Doc" Morad owned it. Now Len Edgerly and Darlene Determan own it.

Bloody Turnip got its name from Ray Whitaker in the 70's. The bank was going to foreclose on some of his property on the mountain. Ray said, "You can't get blood out of a turnip."

Several homes now stand in this area. Up on the ridge is an old bat cave. In another area up a canyon, rock climbers anchor bolts have left their mark on an overhang cliff. To the east on the "CY Canyon" the old "Hogadone Trail" existed that Charles C. Hogadone blazed up the side of the mountain. The original trail ended at Eadsville. Before the Hogadone Trail an older trail went up the mountain following the West Fork of Garden Creek up CY Canyon. The Patee Road also followed this course.

Three deer feed along Garden Creek Road
Photo by Vaughn S. Cronin.

CASPER MOUNTAIN

Continuing east along Garden Creek Road on the left (north) side of the road is a house among the trees. If you look closer you will notice that the house was built around one of the trees.

Photo by Vaughn S. Cronin.

At the foot of the mountain is the first rural subdivision near Casper, where the Blackmore Ranch and the Gothberg Ranch met. By combining the two names it became Gothmore Park.

CAMP DODGE AND FORT CASPAR

Camp Dodge, built in 1865, was a post in the foothills of Casper Mountain that has been forgotten by most, and often neglected in the history books. "Preston B. Plumb, who had been promoted to Lieutenant Colonel of the regiment when Thomas Moonlight was made a full Colonel, set up regimental headquarters at Camp Dodge, four miles to the southeast of Platte Bridge Station (later known as Fort Caspar) on the east side of upper Garden Creek, where there was plenty of water." THE BATTLE OF PLATTE BRIDGE, J.W. Vaughn, University of Oklahoma Press, 1963. Camp Dodge was often confused with Platte Bridge Station. "It was in plain view from it" CASPAR COLLINS, THE LIFE AND EXPLOITS OF AN INDIAN FIGHTER OF THE SIXTIES, Agnes Wright Spring, Columbia University Press, 1927. Camp Dodge was located above a spot where the East and West Forks of Garden Creek join. The soldiers had maneuvers near Garden Creek Falls.

Story has it that the Indians would provoke the soldiers at Camp Dodge, just to get them to shoot their cannon. The Indians would then sell the cannonballs to soldiers at other forts.

On June 3, 1865, there was bloodshed when six Indians appeared across the river at Platte Bridge Station. Colonel Plumb of Co. B, 11th Kansas Cavalry, stationed at Camp Dodge, received a messenger from First Sergeant Samuel B. White from Platte Bridge, reporting that there might be a possible ambush. First Sergeant White ordered a 12-pound howitzer to fire on the Indians. This round crippled two ponies and the Indians took cover behind the nearby rocks. Ten mounted soldiers were dispatched, followed by ten more soldiers on foot. Another Indian horse was wounded as the Indian tried to cut the telegraph line. When the messenger got to Camp Dodge, Colonial Plumb sent ten mounted soldiers of Co. G, 11th Ohio Cavalry and twenty of his unit, Co. B, 11th Kansas Cavalry to follow on foot. Both units crossed the North Platte River and went five miles north. One Indian pony was killed and two Indians were wounded. Half of Plumb's men fell behind and the Indians charged. Luckily, Plumb's soldiers had superior fire power and the Indians fled. Soon, however, sixty Indians charged down Dry Creek (now known as Casper Creek) in an effort to cut them off from the Platte Bridge. The twenty Camp Dodge soldiers that had straggled behind showed up and the Indians fled. Six soldiers followed the Indians that strayed right and were led into an ambush by thirty Indians. Their pistols were empty, and Private W.T. Bonwell of Co. F, 11th Kansas Cavalry and Private Sahlnecker of Co. G, 11th Ohio Cavalry were killed. Night was coming and the soldiers returned to the Platte Bridge Station.

Private Bonwell was buried where he fell and a sandstone monument was erected over the grave on the road leading to the Garden Creek Falls. In 1899 the remains were shipped to Ft. Russell, Wyoming which is now Warren Air Force Base at Cheyenne, Wyoming, and interred at the soldiers cemetery. The monument was removed the same year.

The next month, two other battles were fought within sight of Casper Mountain. Early, on July 26, 1865, Caspar Collins and four other soldiers died at the Battle of Platte Bridge, and later the same day, Sergeant Amos Custard and 22 other men lost their lives at the Battle of Red Buttes (Custard Battle).

CASPER MOUNTAIN

Caspar Collins' father, Lieutenant Colonel William O. Collins, in times previous to the bloodshed on the plains, had written the War Department and raised the Ohio Cavalry to fight in the Civil War. The Ohio Cavalry was quickly reassigned to the frontier because of the aggressive Indian hostilities. In 1861, the Indians took advantage of the fact that fewer white men were on the plains because of the Civil War. Caspar Wever Collins, son of Lieutenant Colonel Collins came west with his father.

Caspar soon became a friend of the Ogallala Sioux and learned to speak their language. Hunting and fishing were great pastimes to the young Collins which helped to supplement the Army rations.

In 1865 Platte Bridge Station was changed to a permanent fort by the recommendation of Col. William O. Collins. The fort was complete with a blacksmith, stores, telegraph station, and housing for 100 men. Louis Guinard had a log store building southeast of his bridge, which was a main crossing on the Oregon Trail. Log buildings made three sides of the square and a stockade for fifty horses made the other side. It could be defended by twenty men and one howitzer.

Trouble started at the fort after the Kansas soldiers arrived. Captain Bretney and the Ohio soldiers had been at Platte Bridge Station for over a year. The Ohio soldiers in celebration, had been drinking whisky and fired a few rounds. Members of a wagon train camped at the bend of the river where Morad Park is now, said they were more afraid of the soldiers than the Indians. The commanders from the two Cavalry units argued over who had the authority to allow the civilians to camp at that spot, and who had authority to be in charge of the fort. This incident would play a role later, even when Caspar was stationed at Sweetwater Station near Independence Rock. Major Anderson of the Kansas Cavalry ordered Collins to protect a wagon train that was heading from Sweetwater Station, toward the fort, (later known as the Battle of Red Butte) even though Lieutenant Collins was not in his chain of command. Collins was a member of the rival company that had caused so much trouble. Major Anderson's own officers were "sick" or had some other excuse not to go into battle. Captain Bretney told Collins not to go but Collins would not disobey an order. He had to borrow a horse since he was just passing through and did not have his own.

The Indians had amassed three-thousand warriors of the Cheyenne, Arapaho and Sioux to finally put an end to the white man. They had chosen Platte Bridge Station because it was one of the main crossings on the Oregon Trail, with the massive Bridge built by Louis Guinard that was 1,000 feet long and 13 feet wide spanning the North Platte River and because of the telegraph line. They would use a few Indians to lure the soldiers into an ambush.

CAMP DODGE AND FORT CASPAR

Collins was told "not to follow the road but go north to the top of the bluff and turn west parallel to the road where it ascended to the main ridge and meet the wagon train. This way he would remain in full sight of the fort and still have a full view of the north." THE BATTLE OF PLATTE BRIDGE, J.W. Vaughn, University of Oklahoma Press, 1963. Instead of staying in sight of the fort, Collins turned north on top of the bluff (the present site of Boatright & Smith) saving at least part of his soldiers. Private George W. McDonald, Private Sebastian Nehring, Private George Camp, and Private Moses Brown also perished with Collins. Collins was last seen when he turned to rescue a fallen soldier and the unfamiliar horse charged directly into the Indians. Collins' body was later found three miles from the battle on Dry Creek. Telegraph wire was wrapped around the body to drag it. He was missing a hand and a foot, the heart had been removed and twenty-four arrows were still in his body.

Later in the day, the wagon train Collins was sent to rescue came into view of the fort under the leadership of Sergeant Custard. Custard was a Civil War Veteran and was not afraid of a few Indians. As soon as the Indians saw the wagons, they attacked. The soldiers tried to circle the wagons but didn't have time. The three wagons were able to get into position, but the west side was open, and vulnerable for attack. They had been unaware of the battle fought earlier, or of the number of Indians that had amassed in the area. Four hours later they were all dead. "Called Red Buttes Fight in the early days in order to convey the impression that the fort was too far away to send aid to the beleaguered wagon train. The name is a misnomer and definitely misleading." THE BATTLE OF PLATTE BRIDGE, J.W. Vaughn, University of Oklahoma Press, 1963. Soldiers watched the battle from the roof of the fort. The soldiers at the fort were all low on ammunition, with less than twenty rounds per soldier. Killed on the wagon train from Co. D 11th Kansas Vol. CAV were: Private William D. Gray, Teamster Martin Green, Private William H. Miller, Private Thomas Powell, Private Samuel Tull, Private Jacob Zinn and Private John R. Zinn. Soldiers found dead from Co. H 11th Kansas Vol. Cavalry were: Sergeant Amos J. Custard, Private Jesse E. Antram, Private William Brown, Private George Heil, Private August Hoppe, Private John Horton, Private William B. Long, Private Ferdinand Schafer, Private Samuel Sproul, Private William West (no body was ever found) and Private Thomas W. Young. Also among those with the wagon train from Co. K 11th Kansas Vol. Cavalry were George Camp and Sebastian Nehring. Also found were Corporal Shrader, Edwin Summers and Private James Bellew (Ballau). Teamsters Rice B. Hamilton 11th OH Cavalry, and Adam Culp 11th Kansas Cavalry were also among the dead.

After this tragedy, Major General G. M. Dodge notified Lieutenant Collins' family back in Ohio. The creek once known as Dry Creek, where Collins' body was found, was renamed Casper Creek. The mountain to the south that had always been called Black Hills, was renamed Casper Mountain. Later, the name of the town that sprang up was given the name of Casper. Platte Bridge Station was also renamed Fort Caspar. Fort Collins already existed in Colorado (named after Caspar Collins' father) and for that reason they used Caspar Collins' first name for the fort and surrounding landmarks.

CASPER MOUNTAIN

The town of Casper was named in 1888, after Caspar Collins, although his name was misspelled with an 'e' instead of the 'a' on General Order number 49 issued November 21, 1865. It has also been said that the Post Office Department in Washington misspelled the name. The fort uses the correct spelling for Caspar.

In 1867 the fort was abandoned and materials were transported to the growing Fort Fetterman. Indians burned what remained soon afterwards. The Reshaw Bridge, at what is now Evansville, was dismantled or burned the same year. Lumber from the bridge was also reused at Fort Fetterman. In 1922, the Casper City Council obtained the land where the fort once stood. In 1931, 21 marble headstones were placed three miles west of the fort in a gully in memory of the fallen soldiers from the Battle of Red Butte. On the hill to the northeast, there used to be the rock letters with CO HB on it. Part of the original message may have been missing as this was seen almost one-hundred years after the naming of Ft Caspar. This had to be in memory of one of the battles fought near Platte Bridge Station. The rock letters are a mystery today.

The exact spot of the Red Butte Battle is unknown and argued by historians. Even soldiers that returned to the site years later had trouble because of the changing terrain, wandering North Platte River, and new construction.

In 1936 Ft Caspar was rebuilt and stands today with a museum and other structures. The Civilian Conservation Corps (CCC) built parking, access roads, planted trees and shrubs. Working near the river, the CCC found piers from the original bridge. "The fort buildings were completed by the WPA in 1936." <u>CASPER, A PICTORIAL HISTORY</u>, Edna Gorrell Kukura and Susan Niethammer True, The Donning Company Publishers,1986.

Volunteers called "Company I" keep the local history alive by staging events at the old fort as well as participating in parades and other civic activities. Also at the fort, Morris Carter takes visitors on wagon tours of the historic area.

Shari Wrasper, May 1981. Photo by Kim Wrasper Cronin.

CAMP DODGE AND FORT CASPAR

Red Cloud would learn from this battle of Platte Bridge. He would be more patient and let more soldiers get into the ambush before he let Crazy Horse do his bidding at the Fetterman Massacre. Photos by Vaughn S. Cronin.

CASPER MOUNTAIN

Below – Photos of the cemetery at Warren Air Force Base of soldiers who fell in battle near Fort Caspar. Photos by Vaughn S. Cronin.

JOHNNY "HAPPY JACK" ALLEN

Along Garden Creek (Circle Drive) near Bloody Turnip, once lived "Happy Jack" Allen. Allen was an early resident and formed the Wyoming Asbestos Company of Casper Mountain. The claim was near Asbestos Turn, located below Mountaineers Mercantile. In 1890 J.B. Smith and J. Allen held claim to a silver mine. Allen also shared a claim with A. C. Bailey (once owner of Bailey School Supply), and had land at Eadsville. Mines John Allen had included: Hidden Treasure Mine, Maud, Phanwaeist, and Amethyst.

A one-time sheriff, Jack also rode as a guard for Wells Fargo in his day. Happy Jack, along with Bill Hobbs, trained the Lady Lancers, a precision riding team of women who participated in parades and other functions. Allen is buried in a steel vault alongside of his dog on the property near Bloody Turnip and below Allen Canyon.

The original Allen home burned in the 1930's. Len Edgerly and Darlene Determan own the property now. It is used as a conference center.

Left, a picture of the Allen resting place. Photo by Vaughn S. Cronin.

CASPER MOUNTAIN

Johnny Allen made history when he married Nellie Smith at the first wedding at the old St. Anthony's Church on July 4, 1900, with Father James Keating officiating The fellow Casper Fire Department members showed up for the occasion. From the Frances Seely Webb Collection; courtesy of the Casper College Library.

Below – A picture of the Allen place. Photo courtesy Art Randall Collection; Casper College Library.

Next two pages – Ruins at the Allen property. Photos by Vaughn S. Cronin.

JOHNNY "HAPPY JACK" ALLEN

Photos by Vaughn S. Cronin.

CASPER MOUNTAIN

Photos by Vaughn S. Cronin.

FRED PATEE

Known as "The King of Asbestos," Fred Patee mined asbestos on Casper Mountain in the 1930's. The material was used by his chimney company at 1014 S. Oak, now zoned primarily as residential. Asbestos was used in lining chimneys for many Casper homes. Patee had several mining claims on the mountain. Today asbestos is being removed from buildings as some types pose a health hazard to people. Asbestos was once also used in shingles, siding, tile and other building material for insulation.

Patee was a self promoter and a strong individual. This caused problems when he met up with another strong individual, Davy Crockett (Great Grandnephew of the famous Davy Crockett). Violence reportedly erupted between the two on more than one occasion. Patee took Crockett to court for assault and battery and won the case.

A ski slope is named after him at the Hogadon Ski Area on Casper Mountain. This slope named in honor of him is one of the few remaining tributes to our disappearing past.

Photo courtesy The Frances Seely Webb Collection/Casper College Library.

CASPER MOUNTAIN

Below are some photos of work being done on the Patee Road up Allen Canyon in 1910. The Patee Road started at the home of John D. Allen.

Photos courtesy of Art Randall Collection/Casper College Library.

PATEE

Photo courtesy of Art Randall Collection/Casper College Library.

Below/Next page – Photos from Russ Launspach; courtesy the Weaver Collection.

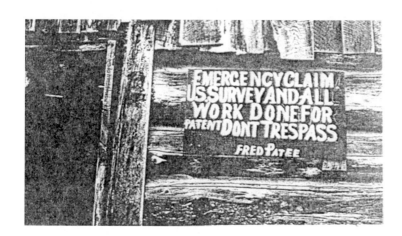

CASPER MOUNTAIN

Below – Pictures of the Patee legacy, from the Weaver collection.

First Asbestos Mill
Built by Fred Patee 1916

Patee's home in 1918
1014 So Oak Casper Wyo

Same place Sept 1922 1014 So Oak St.

CASPER MOUNTAIN

A photo of the Hogadone Trail, up the face of the mountain. This was a shortcut from Casper to Eadsville. Cables helped buggies up the steep trail. Audry Cook McGraugh remembered that the trail was too steep for buggies. They used an alternate route. Three routes up the mountain existed. CY (Allen) Canyon, one up the east end, and the Hogadone Trail. An electric line was later run up the mountain where the old Hogadone Trail once carried traffic. Photo by Vaughn S. Cronin.

CASPER MOUNTAIN

The next point of interest is the house on the north side of Garden Creek Road with the deer in the yard. The deer have become very tame. This is also a good opportunity for photographs. Please note the NO TRESPASSING SIGN! Do NOT venture into their yard. A deer charged a visitor on their property and the person threatened lawsuit. Remember to take precautions when you are around any wild animal.

Following the road east you will see a dirt road that looks like a driveway just 'short' of the road to Garden Creek Falls. This was the start of the Bridle Trail, but now crosses private property.

Photos by Kim Wrasper Cronin

DEFY GRAVITY

On the Garden Creek Falls Road south of the turn into the Rotary Park, at the bottom of the hill, is an interesting spot known as Gravity Hill. Although you can't see this spot, you can experience it. At the bottom of the hill put your car in neutral and roll UP the hill.

I first experienced this in 1970 when the driver of the car, Dwight Harrison, performed this magical feat.

Photo by Kim Wrasper Cronin.

CASPER MOUNTAIN

1920's photograph of Garden Creek Falls by Tom Carrigen;
Wyoming Division of Cultural Resources.

GARDEN CREEK FALLS

Garden Creek Falls are located just off of Garden Creek Road (Circle Drive) at the base of the mountain. Once used as a meeting place by the Indians, they are now closed at 10:00 P.M., and opens again at 7 A.M.

Tragedy struck back in 1895 when a flash flood came roaring down Garden Creek. The story is retold in detail in the CASPER CHRONICLES . . . as well as the Casper Star Tribune July 29, 1967. Four people (Mrs. Newby and her child as well as one Harrison boy and one Harrison girl) lost their lives that night and it was several years before people wanted to camp at the falls again. The Newby child's body was found in a tree. Other people present and who witnessed this tragedy were: Mr. Newby, Samuel Harrison, E. E. Iams, Ed Kerns, James Smith, Fred Seely and Frank Arbiter.

The Casper Rotary Club established Rotary Park, which has picnic tables, and fire containment areas for cooking and campfires. It is a great place to visit and take pictures. Soldiers from the Platte Bridge Station planted flowers below the falls in 1858-67. Later "Garden Creek" got its name.

Below is a picture from 1895, Courtesy of the Carol Mae Wilson Collection.

In July 1996 an 18-year-old man fell to his death climbing the rocks at Garden Creek Falls. A tragic accident like this happens on the average of once every three years involving serious injury or death. You now need a permit to climb the rocks.

CASPER MOUNTAIN

GARDEN CREEK FALLS

Garden Creek Falls has also been the site of weddings, although Natrona County has a very high divorce rate.

Right – There are a series of smaller pools and falls above Garden Creek Falls, as the creek cascades down the mountain. Photos by Vaughn S. Cronin.

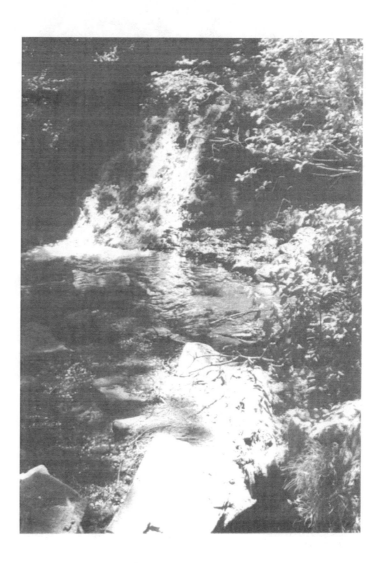

CASPER MOUNTAIN

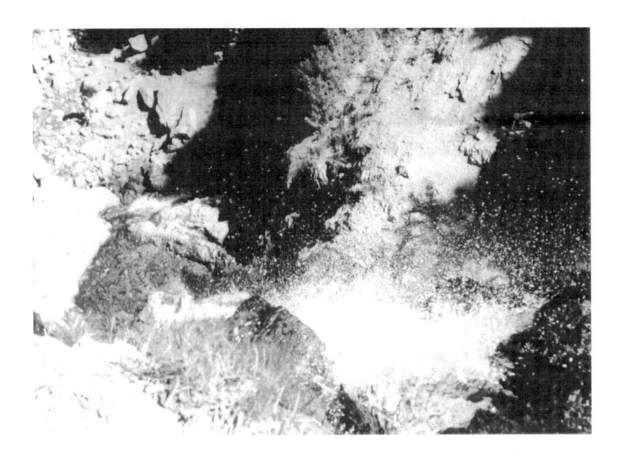

A scene from the top of the falls. Photo by Vaughn S. Cronin.

BRIDLE TRAIL

The Bridle Trail located around and above Garden Creek Falls, was built by the Civilian Conservation Corps (CCC) established in 1933 to help bring an end to the Great Depression during Franklin D. Roosevelt's term as president. It was a Federal Agency established to oversee conservation of natural resources. It provided on the job training to jobless men that were unmarried U.S. citizens between the ages of seventeen and twenty-three years of age. The CCC improved roads, built picnic tables, latrines, fencing, cleared land, and provided assistance as firefighters on Casper Mountain. They also improved the parking area, and buildings, among other tasks at Ft Caspar.

The CCC dissolved when the needs of America shifted from recovering from a depression to crushing an Axis. The Axis was an alliance of Germany and Italy in 1936 which later included Japan, that opposed the American allies in World War II. In the First World War the nations allied against the central powers of Europe; they were Russia, France, Great Britain, and later the United States along with many others.

The CCC was a direct result of the "New Deal" legislation of 1933. Workers were paid $30 a month. Depression dollars went a long way. Photo from Dorothy Reeves Collection.

CASPER MOUNTAIN

The Bridle Trail, built by the Civilian Conservation Corp. (CCC) in the 30's. Photo by Vaughn S. Cronin.

This is a photo across Garden Creek Canyon to the trail east of the falls. Art Randall in a letter dated April 25, 1996 says, "The Hogadone Trail was in the Garden Creek Drainage and probably ran on both the east and west sides. It went by Asbestos Spring up the mountain through Bruce Snedden property."

This is the Hogadone Tram Trail that was a forerunner to the Bridle Trail. The Hogadone Trail ran up the mountain two canyons to the west of the falls, or near Bloody Turnip. Photo by Vaughn S. Cronin.

BRIDLE TRAIL

Here is some of the rock work done on a switchback going up the Bridle Trail. Story has it that the CCC had wooden railings for the blind and others to use along the trail. Pranksters put razor blades in the cracks on top of the rails out of meanness. Photo by Vaughn S. Cronin.

Here is a local resident, a yellow bellied marmot, or (rock chuck), on the Bridle Trail. Photo by Vaughn S. Cronin.

CASPER MOUNTAIN

I always feel at peace with the world on this portion of the Bridle Trail. Photos by Vaughn S. Cronin.

Below – a view of the city from the top of Big Buttress #2.

BRIDLE TRAIL

Splitrock was larger and more magnificent than I had remembered it, so I went back down and got a disposable panoramic camera and walked back up to photograph it. Photos of mine from four different cameras appear in this book. The Bridle Trail goes right through this natural split. Please do not build fires inside or climb it. This is a request from the property owner. Photo by Vaughn S. Cronin.

CASPER MOUNTAIN

Top Right – A cautious deer on the Bridle Trail. Photos by Vaughn S. Cronin.

Signs mark the trail as it loops back down the mountain.

BRIDLE TRAIL

The Bridle Trail crosses Garden Creek just below this small falls. Photos by Vaughn S. Cronin.

Here is a tribute to drivers, machines and insurance claims of the past. Did this car go off of the Hogadone Tram Trail, or a road higher up the mountain?

CASPER MOUNTAIN

Parts of the trail along the east side of the canyon are much wider than the trail up the west side of the drainage. Several people have told me that the CCC built this trail and it has nothing to do with the Hogadone Tram Trail. Photos by Vaughn S. Cronin.

BRIDLE TRAIL

In 1946 a large fire raged above Garden Creek Falls. An earlier fire burned most of the mountain in 1870. This date was determined by counting tree rings. The 100 year cycle for another horrific fire is past due. This monument to one of those fires can be seen along the Bridle Trail. Photo by Vaughn S. Cronin.

CASPER MOUNTAIN

Here are some guidelines about hiking. This could also be used as a guide for four-wheeling, cross-country skiing or a number of other things. Everyone, including myself, have decided with no prior planning to climb something or hike somewhere with no water, bad shoes, the wrong clothes, you name it. Before you know it the terrain is a little worse than you thought it would be, you are sweating, deer flies and mosquitoes are landing on you, the underbrush has scratched your arms and legs, your feet hurt, you feel nauseated, disoriented, buzzards are circling overhead . . .

Before you go on a hike: let someone know where you are going; take water; wear the right clothes, for example, long pants to walk through thick underbrush; and a jacket for cool evenings. Use the "Buddy System" and don't go alone if you can avoid it. Also recommended are: water purifier, a compass, first aid kit, sunscreen, and bug spray. A cellular phone and a navigation system would also be recommended. In this scenario let's say you get hurt on a trail. You can use your navigation system that works off of eight satellites that circle the earth, to give you an exact map point of where you are located. Then use your cellular phone (that also allows help to pinpoint your location) to call 911 for help. Help will arrive a lot faster than if you went on a hike by yourself without telling anyone. You might not see another person for days. A handicapped boy named Kevin Dye was lost on Casper Mountain for approximately one week, although several rescuers searched a large area. The boy was found safe, although most people lost for several days do not survive.

Now back to the Bridle Trail. You can spend two hours or more to walk the whole trail. The Bridle Trail is a complex system of trails around and above Garden Creek Falls. Take a camera. You may see a variety of wildlife, as well as of course, the scenery.

Trails can change for various reasons; erosion, fires, changes in land ownership, landslides, additional new trails, also through disuse. New trees, grass and plants can hide portions of old trails. Many trails show signs of these things. Portions of a trail may be wide enough for a buggy and other spots are barely wide enough for a person. Land owners above the Bridle Trail have paved roads, put up signs, built structures, landscaped etc. If there is a period of several years between your trips, the area may not look the way you remembered it.

Today hikers, rock climbers, mountain bikes as well as horses share the Bridle Trail.

CASPER MOUNTAIN

CASPER MOUNTAIN ROAD

CASPER MOUNTAIN ROAD

Wolcott Street in downtown Casper turns into Casper Mountain Road. Starting the odometer at the intersection of Wyoming Blvd. and Casper Mountain Road (251), head south toward the mountain.

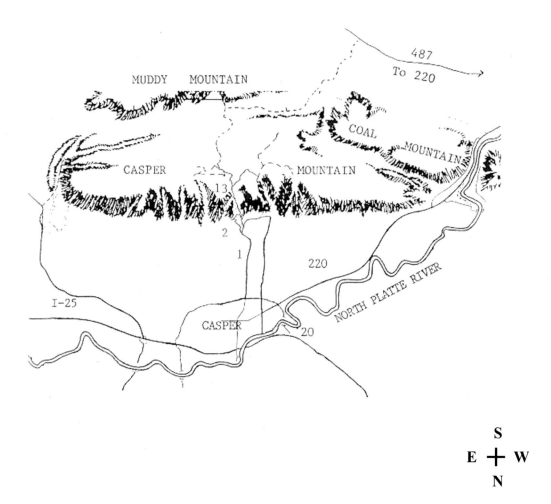

*Note the map is upside down from a normal map. This is to let you orient the map from a Casper location.

1. Site of Dempsey Stables	1.1 mi.	9. Rock Climbing	4.5 mi.
2. Elkhorn Subdivision	1.7 mi.	10. Site of Brookside Inn	7.1 mi.
3. Intersection WY 252	1.9 mi.	11. Site of Dixie Lodge	7.4 mi.
4. First Curve	2.6 mi.	12. Site of Thunder Bolt	7.4 mi.
5. Lathrop Turn	2.8 mi.	Ski Course	5.7 mi.
6. Wylan Turn	3.0 mi.	13. Asbestos Spring	5.6 mi.
7. Hairpin Curve	3.4 mi.	14. Mountaineer's Merc.	5.7 mi.
8. Lookout Point	4.2 mi.	15. Junction	5.9 mi.

CASPER MOUNTAIN ROAD TO THE HOGADON TURN OFF

Heading south toward the mountain, the road climbs Montgomery Hill, named after Matt Montgomery, who was a rancher at the foot of the mountain and one of the first investors in asbestos stocks. His property was later known as the Kerr Place. The cut for the road is known as the Dugway, dug out of the hill with teams. The road was opened August 28, 1962 at a cost of $588,638.00.

The highway passes the Dempsey Stable site, on the east side of the road (left), and parallels the remains of the equestrian path (right). An old rock quarry sits abandoned, also on the west (right). The Dempsey Stable Site is marked number 1 on the map on the previous page.

As the steep climb starts, you will pass the turn to Garden Creek Road. Lookout Point is marked number 2, Asbestos Spring and Road is marked number 3, and Mountaineer's Mercantile is marked number 4.

Photo shows the site of Dempsey Stables, now a private residence. People used to rent horses here and ride up the Bridle Trail near Garden Creek Falls.

Photo by Vaughn S. Cronin.

CASPER MOUNTAIN

An Old Postcard View of Casper Mountain.
Photo by Tom Carrigen; courtesy of Eleanor Carrigen.

The same road today.
Photo by Vaughn S. Cronin.

ELKHORN CANYON

Elkhorn Canyon is the second canyon east of the Casper Mountain Road. Casper's first waterworks used the water from Elkhorn Creek for its facility. The town of Evansville has also used Elkhorn Creek for a source of good clean water. Much of this canyon is on private property, so you need to check before you tramp over the countryside in this area.

Elkhorn Creek flows east from the central portion of the mountain through the former site of the Pratt Ranch and the Casper Country Club area.

Mining activity in Elkhorn Canyon started anew in 1897 when Dr. J.F. Leeper reopened the old "Galena Queen." The strike was made at a depth of 85 feet in the shaft, and the galena ore shipped to Denver for assay. The assayer's certificate indicated $1,012.83 per ton. Within an hour of the news people rushed to the mountain to stake claims for themselves and anyone else they could think of. After the claims had been legally recorded, the news came back that there was a mistake on the assay; it should have been $3.10 per ton. The mining activity abruptly ended.

In 1972 some friends were hiking in the canyon when they spotted a hermit. This filthy creature would peer at them from afar and then he would disappear; only to reappear a few moments later on a different level in the canyon. He never let the hikers get within 100 yards of him.

Aerial photo shows highway up the north face of mountain. Elkhorn Canyon is two canyons to the left (east) of Hairpin Curve. Garden Creek is to the right (west) of the road. Photo courtesy Dana Van Burgh, with pilots Judy Logue and Linda Wackwitz; courtesy of the Wyoming Field Science Foundation.

CASPER MOUNTAIN

The Arnold cabin west of Elkhorn Creek, on the north face of the mountain, still partially stands. It is close to the opening of a mine. A headstone, with the name of John Arnold, stands near a cabin. This is adjacent to the burn area of the Elkhorn Canyon fire of 1994. John Arnold mined for copper and "paint rock" at this site. He never sold any ore. Mines he had claim to included: Cloud Burst, Copper Glover, Cross, and Lead Lode.

Although a confirmed bachelor, Arnold had women who loved him. In 1962, Dave Olson found love letters written to John Arnold from a woman who wrote him most of his life. Peggy Simson Curry, in her poetry later referred to these letters.

The Arnold Cabin. Art Randall made an archaeological excavation of the floor and surrounding area, finding buttons and other artifacts. Photo courtesy Art Randall collection/ Casper College Library.

John Arnold's sheep wagon near the Lathrop Cabin. Sheep wagons were first built in Rawlins, Wyoming in 1887. Arnold was the winter caretaker for the Lathrops. He would run a flag up a flag-pole to show his well being. Photo courtesy Art Randall Collection/Casper College Library.

ELKHORN CANYON

One of John Arnold's old mines. During the Elkhorn fire of 1994 the mine still had snow and cool air inside. Photo courtesy Art Randall Collection/Casper College Library.

Photo courtesy Art Randall Collection/Casper College Library.

Another view of John Arnold's resting place. It was discovered that the grave had been dug up when kids cruising CY Avenue held Arnold's head out of their car window. This proved to be very painful for the perpetrators for the rest of their lives. Photo courtesy Art Randall Collection/Casper College Library.

CASPER MOUNTAIN

Elkhorn Stage Station. Photo courtesy Art Randall Collection/Casper College Library.

Needle Eye, at Elkhorn Canyon. Photo by Vaughn S. Cronin.

HAIRPIN CURVES

The present road up Casper Mountain has several hairpin curves. The scar on the mountain from the present road is clearly visible for many miles from the face of the mountain. The first small curve is Bessemer Turn. There is a wide area that you can pull off of and take pictures like the one below of the frozen Garden Creek Falls.

Photo by Kim Wrasper Cronin.

The first hairpin curve is called Lathrop Turn. The road to the east goes to the old Lathrop Cabin, still owned by the family. The fault on the face of the mountain runs between Lathrop Turn and Wylan Turn further up the mountain. In the early days, parents would have their children get out and help push the car up the mountain, while they steered and restarted stalled engines.

Lathrop Turn photo by Vaughn S. Cronin.

CASPER MOUNTAIN

Lathrop Cabin, Photo by Vaughn S. Cronin. This photo won 2nd Place in Historical Color at the 1996 Central Wyoming Fair & Rodeo.

Photo by Tom Carrigen; courtesy Eleanor Carrigen.

The most famous hairpin curve on the mountain is called Hairpin Turn. The photo above shows a Needle Eye on the cliff. The photo on the next page is a present day photo of what is called Hairpin Turn, or Layman's Corner named after Fred Layman who built a house above it. In the 1920's it was a one-way dirt track.

HAIRPIN CURVES

Above Hairpin Curve, Fred and Brenda Layman built a beautiful museum of a home with European antiques. Two grand pianos sat on an interior patio that doubled as a stage for concerts. Tom Carrigen would use his operatic voice as Brenda Layman accompanied on the piano. Tom Carrigen also sang at funerals and weddings, as well as other civic activities.

Many other gifted people performed at the house on Hairpin Turn. In 1958 the Layman's smelled gas. Mr. Layman lit a match to find the leak and found it. The house with all of the antiques burned. The second house reportedly has an elevator.

Mr. Layman decided to have a cemetery on the property for those who would like their ashes interred on the mountain. There is little to see at the cemetery for a tourist.

West Magoon says that a student or disciple of Frank Lloyd Wright designed this house.

Photo by Kim Wrasper Cronin.

CASPER MOUNTAIN

Although officially completed in 1962, the Casper Mountain Road was in existence in the 1920's. Fuel systems on the old cars were not made for the steep grade up the mountain, so the cars would have to go up the mountain backwards, so that the engine could get fuel.

Photo by Ken Ball; from the Asbell Collection.

LOOKOUT POINT

Above – A 1940 postcard view of Lookout Point by Tom Carrigen; courtesy Wyoming Division of Cultural Resources, Department of Commerce. Below is the present day view. Photo by Vaughn S. Cronin. Rails are not present along the entire route because they cause snowdrifts. The snow removal equipment can't shoot the snow over the rails. Notice in the bottom picture how much the hill has been excavated to widen Lookout Point.

CASPER MOUNTAIN

Present day photo from Look Out Point by Vaughn S. Cronin. The present day photo could not achieve the same angle that Tom Carrigen had, due to lack of height. Tom Carrigen had a lofty hillside to stand on for his photo. Mr. Asbell told me that Lookout point was enlarged in 1962 when Asbell Construction completed the present road.

LOOKOUT POINT

Lookout point is a picturesque spot on the main road up the face of Casper Mountain. Old pictures show the changes in Casper over the years and how it has grown.

Hang-gliders use Lookout Point as a jump-off. You can watch them as you picnic at Garden Creek Falls, located below Lookout Point.

1950's Photo from Look Out Point by Tom Carrigen; courtesy of Eleanor Carrigen.

CASPER MOUNTAIN

This rock was picked up by the tree as it grew. Photo by Vaughn S. Cronin.

Winter on Casper Mountain. This Photo by Kim Wrasper Cronin won Honorable Mention at the 1996 Wyoming State Fair in Douglas.

LOOKOUT POINT

This Tom Carrigen photo from the 1920's shows a very interesting tree. Now what remains of this tree looks like a "Dragon Head." Courtesy Wyoming Division of Cultural Resources.

Below – Casper, from Casper Mountain. From the Bernfeld collection; Courtesy the American Heritage Center, University of Wyoming.

CASPER MOUNTAIN

Kelly Moore scales a challenging spot on Casper Mountain. Photo courtesy the Moore Collection.

ROCK CLIMBING

Rock climbers have many opportunities on Casper Mountain, although a lot of good places are on private land. A good book on the subject is HIGH PLAINS CLIMBS, A GUIDE TO THE CASPER MOUNTAIN AREA, 1983 by Patrick Parmenter, Kelly Moore, and Arno U. Ilgner. In the book are maps of locations that are available.

One area, called Red Rocks, is just past Lookout Point. Above the Casper Mountain Road is the Upper Limestone. Garden Creek Falls has some good cliffs to climb also. Some of the rock is very brittle and therefore the holds should be tested to avoid serious problems. Do not climb Split Rock. The owner wants to maintain the beauty of the magnificent spot.

Because Casper Mountain is close to town, climbers can enjoy the mountain in the afternoon, or evenings after work. These shorter climbs can get the enthusiast prepared to tackle larger tasks around the world.

James Doherty at Back Country Mountain Works in the Sunrise Shopping Center is very helpful at explaining how to get to these natural wonders as well as mountain bike trails, hiking trails, and cave exploring.

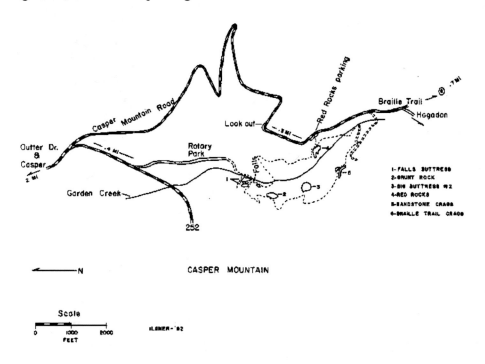

Map courtesy of Arno U. Ilgner. From the book HIGH PLAINS CLIMBING, A GUIDE TO THE CASPER MOUNTAIN AREA, 1983.

CASPER MOUNTAIN

Rock climbing differs from mountain climbing in that the rock climber has more control over the elements. A mountain climber may endeavor to climb a great height that will take several days to scale. Lack of oxygen and bitter cold can end the triumph of a mountain climber. A rock climber can go out for a few hours, and if it looks too cold or windy, wait for another day.

This anchor bolt has been an aid to climbers for many years.
Photo by Vaughn S. Cronin.

SNOWSHOEING

Some of the remote cabins on Casper Mountain are accessed by snowshoes, ATV, cross-country skiing, and snowmobile.

Before snowshoeing, make sure you are not trespassing on private property. Snowshoeing requires very little training or technique to learn. Always let someone know where you are going. Take a first aid kit and some water with you when you go. Wear appropriate clothing and take extra clothes with you in a day pack or back pack.

Snowshoes have been around for nearly 6,000 years. It appears that snowshoes made their way from Asia to our North American continent.

Above is a picture of the old Brookside Inn, now a popular parking area for rock climbers. The original smaller building was white. Later, the building pictured, was enlarged even further by adding a dance floor on the back, and extending the structure to the south. Clarence and Pearl Littlefield owned the Brookside Inn which burned in the late 1950's. The cabin area in the valley below has another Littlefield structure called Killkare. This valley above Garden Creek Falls has some of the earliest cabins on the mountain.

CASPER MOUNTAIN

A beautiful snow covered morning. Notice the foundation of the Brookside Inn site (middle left). Photos by Vaughn S. Cronin.

Below – Bernadine Reed at Killkare August 1996.

CASPER MOUNTAIN

Part of the Reed complex. Photos by Vaughn S. Cronin.

CASPER MOUNTAIN

Below – Shovels like these were hooked to horses or mules for mining or digging.
Photo by Vaughn S. Cronin.

ASBESTOS SPRING & ASBESTOS MINE

A now missing landmark on Casper Mountain, is the Asbestos Spring. Many an overheated car or truck would stop there. People would drink from the cool mountain spring once noted for its good drinking water, filling containers to take home with them. Late in the '60's, the Asbestos Spring was shut off for public safety reasons. The spring was located on a hairpin turn, high up on Casper Mountain, 7.7 miles from Casper,

The Asbestos Mine is located near the old spring up the dirt road heading southwest from the old spring site. The mine is on private property and you should ask the O'Quinns before wandering into the old shaft.

"The Last" Asbestos Mine – Photo by Vaughn S. Cronin.

This mine opening is in the O'Quinn's yard. Their home was built using parts from the old McKinley School. The large building seen in later pages once hid this mine inside its walls.

Rumor has it that this eighty-five foot mine shaft never hit any ore. It was said to have been "salted" with asbestos to help sell the property. This mine was different from the surrounding mines in that it was the only mine not connected to the others, it is the only opening that was not filled back in, and Art Randall found no sign of asbestos in this mine.

CASPER MOUNTAIN

Left – Asbestos Spring in the early days. It was built by the Jaycee's in 1944. From the Chuck Morrison Collection; courtesy Casper College Library. Right – The material from the Asbestos Spring discarded and reused as a culvert. Photo by Vaughn S. Cronin.

A winter picture of Asbestos Turn Today. Photo by Vaughn S. Cronin.

ASBESTOS SPRING & ASBESTOS MINE

Historic photo of Asbestos Mine Area.

In 1890, J.C. Hogadone discovered asbestos on Casper Mountain. By 1891, asbestos had been found over a vast area. Fibers ranged from two inches, to over ten inches in length. Local reports said that the quality was comparable to the best from other areas around the world. One hundred claims were staked covering over three hundred acres.

Men like Charles W. Eads, Charles C. Hogadone, and Matt Montgomery had a stake in the asbestos claims. Around 1905, A. E. Minium promoted companies and stocks that netted the promoter several thousand dollars. Mr. Minium did not use the money for research and development and soon had a bad reputation for his fraudulent methods. Investors and new promoters turned sour. Lawsuits ensued and the property was lost to the attorney.

In the 1930's, Fred Patee successfully mined asbestos for chimney insulation. In the 1980's, asbestos was being removed from public buildings as a health hazard for cancer.

CASPER MOUNTAIN

Old picture of road. Arrow points to old mill building.

ASBESTOS SPRING & ASBESTOS MINE

Left – Picture of old mine road.
Historic Photo

Right – Same road today.
Photo by Vaughn S. Cronin.

 A scenic road was blazed up the mountain to the mines and the top of the mountain. New homesteads, cabins, and picnic areas followed. Wild Oats Lane was near the mines, with a beautiful view of Casper. Some of the early residents "sewed their wild oats" on Wild Oats Lane.

CASPER MOUNTAIN

Picture of Asbestos Headquarters. At one time this building was Casper's first court house from 1895 to 1909.

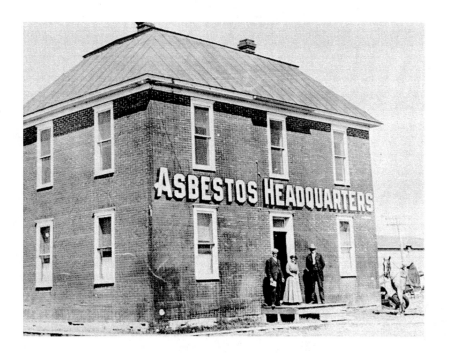

The courthouse that replaced the old building was located at the end of Center Street. Today that location would be in the center of the street in front of the present courthouse. Completed in 1908, it stood until 1940. The Carey family previously owned the land for the site. Many in town opposed this site. North Casper did not exist before Pathfinder Dam was built because that area periodically flooded from the North Platte River. Courtesy the Wyoming State Cultural Division.

ASBESTOS SPRING & ASBESTOS MINE

This is another picture of the courthouse completed in 1908. It is partially hidden behind the Townsend Hotel sign. It stood in the middle of Center Street. The area north of the courthouse was accessed via a circular drive around the building. Notice that the cupola is missing from the top of the building. Perhaps the building was being torn down in this picture.

In 1938, Casper's three biggest hotels: the Henning, Gladstone and Townsend Hotels, were at Center and First Street. The courthouse stood at the end of Center Street. In the early days women didn't walk down the west side of Center Street where the bars were. The present (third) courthouse was part of the Works Projects Administration (WPA) project under Franklin D. Roosevelt, in the late 1930's. Photo from the Seymour S. Bernfeld Collection; Courtesy American Heritage Center, University of Wyoming.

CASPER MOUNTAIN

ASBESTOS SPRING & ASBESTOS MINE

Previous page – Asbestos Mill where O'Quinn's home now sits. Courtesy O'Quinn Collection. Right – Ruth Joy Hopkins painting of same building. Painting owned by Warren Weaver. The "Last Mine" was inside this structure.

An old ore cart sits abandoned at Asbestos Mine sites. The Hogadone Tram Trail ran to this area. Photos by Vaughn S. Cronin.

Remains of old mill near water tank shown on previous page. Stories of a ghost wearing a gray shirt and red suspenders wandering in this area have been told by some of the "old timers."

CASPER MOUNTAIN

Top & bottom – Trees force their way through tailings from the asbestos mines to reclaim their spot on the mountain. Note the lack of trees in the photo two pages prior.

Right – Picture of the Glory Hole. It has since been filled in for safety. All of the ore from the surrounding mines was extracted through this hole. Note picture two pages earlier. Photos by Vaughn S. Cronin.

MOUNTAINEER'S MERCANTILE

The Mountaineer's Mercantile is located just beyond the last hairpin turn after you reach the top of the mountain. The Mercantile is a convenient place to rent cross country ski gear, mountain bikes, or just stop for a snack. The building was once known as the WA-WA Lodge. In the book <u>WYOMING, A GUIDE TO IT'S HISTORY, HIGHWAYS, AND PEOPLE</u>, Oxford University Press, New York, 1941, it states "Wa-Wa Lodge, 8 mi., serves meals in season and has a dance floor."

Nils Fougstedt passed land down to his brother Oly who lived near the Wa-Wa Lodge. Travelers would often stop by to warm up and talk with Oly on their way up or down the mountain. One winter evening Jim Forsling stopped by. He had skied to town and was returning to his home at Crimson Dawn. Oly had a big tube type radio that he listened to. Oly told Jim that a bad storm was coming in and that he should just sleep there until it passed. Jim assured him that it wasn't that far to get home and that he would be all right. That was the last time anyone saw Jim alive. Neal Forsling would find his frozen body near their home a few days later. Jim Forsling died March 3, 1942.

During the winter of '49, Ken Ball took a "Weasel" (an Army National Guard Track Vehicle) up the mountain with supplies for Oly. Oly was a little put out that anyone thought that he might be in any danger and would not take any of the groceries, although he did keep the bottle of whisky and the chew.

Photo by Vaughn S. Cronin.

CASPER MOUNTAIN

A picture of the track vehicle used to rescue Oly. Pictured are members of the Army National Guard. Photo by Ken Ball; courtesy of the Ken Ball family.

Story has it that Oly and Nils Fougstedt were "in cahoots" with some of the local law enforcement. The cabin they had was northwest of the Wa-Wa Lodge and they could see the city of Casper. When the revenuers would start to go up the mountain to arrest anyone with an illegal still, a red light would be placed on top of the police station in town. The still would disappear by the time the revenuers would arrive.

MOUNTAINEER'S MERCANTILE

A view from the Mercantile looking north. Photo by Vaughn S. Cronin.

A 1937 ad from the Wa-Wa Lodge (famous for their pancakes, too). Notice that later pictures show the addition to the building on the west (right) end. Picture on next page by Eleanor Carrigen, (it has been debated that Muriel Street may have been the photographer) is of Jack (J.R.) Cummings, original homesteader and a picture of the Wa-Wa Lodge with the addition. Cummings and Tom Carrigen (who took some of the historic pictures used in this book), were both projectionists at the America Theatre, complete with six piece orchestra, in the silent film days. Cummings died Feb 13, 1963. Photos & Ad courtesy the Wenger Collection.

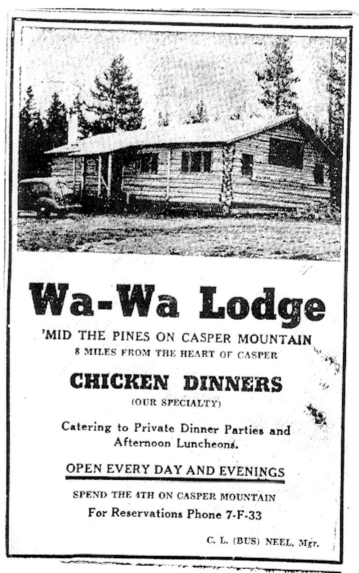

CASPER MOUNTAIN

CASPER MOUNTAIN

THE ROAD TO HOGADON

CASPER MOUNTAIN

Photo by Vaughn S. Cronin 1996.

MAP OF THE ROAD TO HOGADON

Starting at the "Y" in the road just south of the Mountaineer's Mercantile, take a right turn. This is the road that leads to Hogadon Ski area.

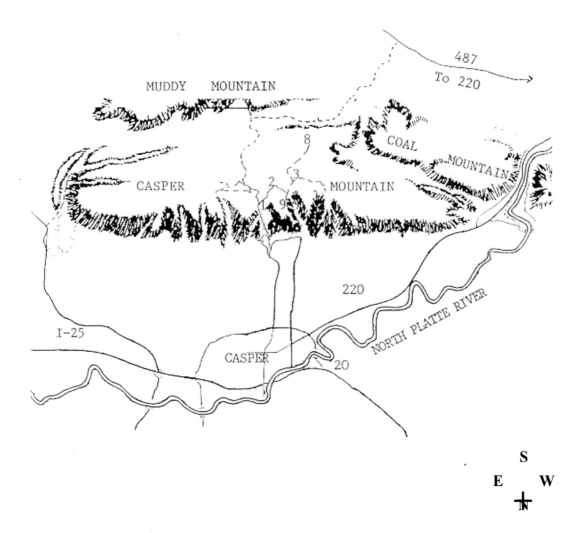

* Note that this is an upside down map. This will help orient you from a Casper location.

1. Street Car	0.2 mi.	5. Eadsville	1.4 mi.
2. Mtn. Top Baptist Assembly Camp	0.7 mi.	6. Camp Sacajawea	1.4 mi.
		7. WW II Beacon	1.7 mi.
3. K2 Tower	0.7 mi.	8. Adams Archery Range	3.0 mi.
4. Micro Rd/Co 504	1.3 mi.	9. Hogadon Ski Area	1.5 mi.

STREET CAR

On the road to Hogadon, about .2 miles from the Hogadon Junction, on the north side, is a street car. Story has it that in the 1940's the streetcar or trolley was brought from Denver, Colorado to Casper Mountain. Clayton Peterson from E. E. Peterson Construction Co., Don Perry, and Bob Hardesty paid $50 for the street car in Denver and brought it up by truck. The last one to get married was to get the street car. Bob Hardesty was the last one married, but Don Perry has the property taxes in his name.

Graffiti from the old days can still be seen on the inside of the walls. This street car was one of the last ones used in Denver before they discontinued use of the system.

Street Car photos by Vaughn S. Cronin.

DAVY CROCKETT

David B. Crockett, the great grandnephew of the famous Davy Crockett, once roamed Casper Mountain. He had a claim on the mountain known as the "Moonshine Lode" and a cabin that was known as "Suits Me." Under the floor of this cabin was a shaft that led to the vanadium mine. The false floor in front of his stove allowed him to work through the winter months.

Davy had a feud with Fred Patee since both of them had claims on the same land. One famous story tells of the two of them having a shoot-out over a theft. Both of them thought they had killed the other one in the exchange of gunfire, and so they both went to town to turn themselves in.

Crockett died January 31, 1937 at seventy-five years of age. He is buried on top of Casper Mountain.

Below, pictures of "Suits Me." Photo by Vaughn S. Cronin.

Dean Meckling brought food to Crockett each Friday in Crockett's later years. Meckling later gave the land to Bess Opal Allen in the early 1940's. She gave it back to the Meckling's in the 1970's.

CASPER MOUNTAIN

Right – Another view of "Suits Me."

Below – The unmarked grave of Davy Crockett of Casper Mountain fame. The land owner wants this spot kept a secret so that everyone can "rest in peace." Photos by Vaughn S. Cronin.

DAVY CROCKETT

Right – Warren "Buck" Weaver stands next to the entrance of the "Moonshine Lode." Vanadium was mined around 1910. Photos by Vaughn S. Cronin.

Left – The last remaining sign of the 1870 fire at the Crockett place. This fire destroyed most of Casper Mountain. Tree rings were used to date this fire.

CASPER MOUNTAIN

Above – Tom Carrigen photo of Crockett family. Davy is on the far left; Courtesy the Sam & Laurie Weaver Collection.

Right – The sign for the Crockett homestead. Photo by Vaughn S. Cronin.

CAMP SACAJAWEA

Camp Sacajawea is located on the road to the Hogadon Ski Area. It is named after the "Bird Woman" who led the Lewis and Clark Expedition through the new uncharted land in 1805.

Historians disagree about where she is buried. A sign exists in Fort Washakie, Wyoming near the local cemetery marking her grave. T. A. Larson, in his book HISTORY OF WYOMING, 1978 states, "Visitors are sometimes told that a grave at Fort Washakie is the burial place of Sacajawea of the Lewis and Clark expedition, when most scholars agree that Sacajawea's grave is in South Dakota." It is said that Sacajawea died at Fort Washakie in 1884 at 86 years of age. She is buried with her son Baptiste, and nephew Basil, in a Shoshone cemetery. The reader will have to decide if anyone really knows where Sacajawea is buried.

The camp is used by the Girl Scouts. The Girl Scouts were first organized in Casper in 1922. Mr. and Mrs. P.C. Nicolaysen donated land on Casper Mountain for the camp.

On November 7, 1953 Lady Olave Baden-Powell, founder of the Girl Guides in England (Girl Scouts in America) visited Casper. Mary Hester Nicolaysen started a money raising campaign to bring Lady Baden-Powell to speak. Many interested parents from around the state arrived for the occasion.

Pictured are: Peggy Hoover, Lady Baden-Powell, Mildred Hoover, and daughter Kathy Hoover, cochairman for the Chief Guide's visit. Courtesy Mildred Hoover.

CASPER MOUNTAIN

Sacajawea, who was known by her people as the "Boat Launcher," was misunderstood by Lewis and Clark, who called her the "Bird Woman." She was hired by Lewis and Clark, from 1804-06, to lead them west, into the new uncharted frontier. Sacajawea was a Shoshone Indian who was stolen by Mandan Indians and taken to North Dakota. She was won in a gambling game by her new husband, Charbonneau. She carried her two month old son, Baptiste, on her back as she guided the Lewis and Clark Expedition. When she got to her people she got fresh horses and provisions for the expedition west. "Without her wisdom and fortitude, and ability to make friends with the Indians, the expedition would have failed. She taught how to live in the wilderness, and nurse them back to health with herbs," Mae Urbanek, WYOMING PLACE NAMES, Johnson Publishing Co., Boulder, CO, 1967.

The Girl Scouts admire and emulate the kindness and leadership that Sacajawea possessed in her way of life. Girls enjoy horseback ridding, archery, cooking outdoors games, songs, stories, and camping out in tents during the summer at Camp Sacajawea.

TOWER

Southwest of Hogadon on a dirt road near the Micro Road, is a tall tower once used as a World War II beacon. It is on private property. Don't get caught climbing it! From the top of the tower you can see the Pedro Mountains, Ferris Mountains, Whiskey Peak, Green Mountain, Rattlesnake Mountains, Coal Mountain, Granite Mountains, Oil Mountain, Pine Mountain, Muddy Mountain, Freezout Hills, Shirley Mountains, Elk Mountain, and the Bighorns. Another similar tower exists on the east end of the mountain by fire marker number six.

The tower was used to warn pilots of the gas powered B-24's and B-17's of the danger of the impending mountain. The low flying planes had problems gaining altitude in the high winds in the area. Planes did crash on the mountain, one west of Eadsville and one in the eagle sanctuary.

Photo by Vaughn S. Cronin.

Due to national security during wartime, the pieces of the crashed planes were quickly recovered. A base photographer handled all of the photography of a sensitive nature. Not enough instructors were available for the four engine bombers. Each plane had an eight to twelve man crew.

Pilots came from training in a coastal region before they arrived at Casper for an additional ten to twelve weeks of mountain training. From here they went straight to Europe, or the Asiatic War Theater. The B-17's and B-24's played a major role in ending World War II.

CASPER MOUNTAIN

Mountain flowers and mountain ranges, on the road to the Adams Archery Range.
Photo by Vaughn S. Cronin.

ADAMS ARCHERY RANGE

Photos by Vaughn S. Cronin

On the road to Hogadon (about 3 miles after the fork in the road to Hogadon) is the sign for the Robert L. Adams Memorial Archery Range. R.L. Adams, a former Park Director, died December 4, 1989 at the age of 59. Take Micro Road to get to the range. It is a challenging course, and arrows can get lost or found in the trees behind the targets. It is a realistic place to practice your skills as an archer.

Hunting is prohibited in the archery range. Broadhead arrows are also prohibited. Anyone over sixteen years of age needs a range use pass issued by the Natrona County Parks Board.

CASPER MOUNTAIN

Right – A target left behind by an archer. Photos by Vaughn S. Cronin.

Left – Photo of the Mystery Mine on the way to archery range. It earned its name when two carloads of ore shipped from Casper were never seen again.

ADAMS ARCHERY RANGE

COPPEROPOLIS

Copperopolis was a mining community a short distance southeast of Eadsville, at the headwater of Little Red Creek. The 50 inhabitants lived in what is now an area near the archery range. In 1988-92 Art Randall did an archaeological excavation of the area and wrote COPPEROPOLIS, A GHOST TOWN ON TOP OF CASPER MOUNTAIN, 1992. Several small artifacts were catalogued and given to Jean Marie Speas Niethammer, the owner of the land.

As late as the 1970's a person could pick up pieces of copper lying on top of the ground; today the ground is picked clean. Little is left of the old mining site.

Picture of hoist house at Copperopolis. In 1988-92 Art Randall and a crew did an archaeological excavation of the dirt floors of the building and surrounding area. Photo courtesy Art Randall.

Building 'A' at Copperopolis during excavation in July, 1992. Photo courtesy Art Randall.

CASPER MOUNTAIN

Dane Mattern at building 'A' at Copperopolis in August 1990. Photo courtesy Art Randall.

COPPEROPOLIS

Below is a 1906 picture of the miners at Copperopolis, a short distance from Eadsville. From right to left are Shorty Hiney, George Myers, John Irwin, unidentified, and Wil Cook, probably at the Blue Cap Mine. This area had been mined before and abandoned in 1890. Photograph by Audry Cook McGraugh, from the Bernadine Reed collection.

CASPER MOUNTAIN

Mining activity at Copperopolis. Photos by Vaughn S. Cronin.

CASPER MOUNTAIN

Here is a quick timetable of mining activity on the mountain:

1890	–	J.B. Smith and John D. Allen hit silver ore at $666/ton.
1890 – Sept	–	J.C. Hogadone finds asbestos.
1891 – July	–	Over 100 asbestos claims; Messers, Eads, Hogadone, Montgomery. Also Galena with Jack Currier
Aug	–	Henry Zahn mineralogist from Chicago "You have the perfect formation for asbestos, and the quality is as good as that of the Canadian Mines also gold and coal."
Sept	–	Zahn has 30 day option on 2 asbestos claims.
Oct	–	Zahn switched to copper. Plans are made to build a railroad up the mountain.
1892 – March	–	Zahn Syndicates have 28' shaft, traces of two copper claims. "Cross Fox" and "Blue Cap" (an Abe Nelson lease).
1895-96	–	Casper Mountain Mining Co., J.L. Garner, president; John D. Allen, vice president; F.H. Burrow, secretary, with Capitol Stock at $10,000. All shares sold out at $1.00/share.
1905-6	–	Mining resumes and ends at Blue Cap.

Charles Eads, Courtesy Pioneer Museum.

CASPER MOUNTAIN

EADSVILLE

South of Hogadon Ski Area and northeast of the archery range lies the area known as Eadsville. Once known as a mining town in the 1880's, there is little left now except the spring of ice cold water that once was the center of town, and the scars from old mine shafts and other mining activity. A gold strike was made on Casper Mountain in 1890. Businessmen, cowboys, laborers and the like quit their jobs in search of fast riches. Reports boasted that the claims would be richer than the Anaconda in Montana. Miners looked until 1895 when the rich veins were found to be asbestos and other minerals.

Miners were looking at pegmatite. Pegmatite is formed when molten rock cools very slowly and minerals solidifying at different temperatures clump together making for some very interesting looking crystals. Unfortunately the quality and quantity was not large enough for profitable business enterprise.

The old town of Eadsville covered 20 acres of land on top of Casper Mountain. In 1880 it was filed on by Charles W. Eads and was platted and surveyed for a stamp mill. Gold, silver, lead, galena, copper, and asbestos mines were opened up in all directions from the town.

Cal Cook, mining engineer and geologist in the Hidden Treasure mine.

Excitement mounted in January 1891 when S.A. (Jack) Currier received news back from Omaha on some ore he had sent in showing 33 ounces of silver and 82 percent lead. On the strength of this, later in the year a telegram came in from Deadwood, South Dakota, requesting six carloads per day be shipped to the mills there. Hundreds of claims were filed and the town grew in size. Because of snow, the mines had not been properly opened, and production was at a standstill.

Later news came back that the quality of the ore was not sufficient to continue the cost outlay for production and transportation of the ore. Exodus ensued in 1897.

Previous page is a photo of the TB Recuperation Camp at Eadsville in 1925. Photo by Tom Carrigen; courtesy Casper College Library.

CASPER MOUNTAIN

The town was named after Charles W. Eads. C.W. Eads is credited for being the second man to locate in Casper with Mr. Merritt being the first settler. Charles W. Eads, name appeared in the NATRONA COUNTY TRIBUNE, May 13, 1908: "C.W. Eads, who carries the reputation of a successful horse thief, will do time in the penitentiary for a theft committed in Big Horn County." Other mining included the head of Hat Six and Goose Creeks, the Galena Queen at the head of Elkhorn Creek, and numerous other spots on the mountain including Copperopolis near Eadsville.

Feldspar is still mined near Eadsville today! The feldspar is ground up and the resulting glaze is used for the shiny glaze found on drinking glasses, bathtubs, stoves, refrigerators and abrasives. The blue feldspar is used in the glaze found in dentures. The Denver Post November 25, 1956, stated, "Asbestos and gold deposits didn't pay, so Casper Mountain's wealth slumbered until the big denture rush of 1956 began."

Below is an 1890 picture of C.W. Eads (right). Frances Seely Webb Collection; courtesy Casper College Library.

EADSVILLE

Below is a picture of George Myers and John Irwin in the Hidden Treasure Mine Tunnel. From the collection of Mrs. Nellie (Cal) Cook, as found in the Frances Seeley Webb Collection, Casper College Library.

Later mining on the mountain included a chromium mine from an area southwest of the Lions Camp during World War II. Deposits were too small, even under the extreme urgency of wartime, to justify mining. The feldspar mine near Camp Sacajawea and a county rock crushing quarry near Bear Trap Meadow are the only mines operating sporadically on the mountain today. Below is a picture of the feldspar mine still in operation. Photo by Vaughn S. Cronin.

CASPER MOUNTAIN

Although not recorded in Casper Mountain History, unscrupulous miners would place a quantity of gold in a scatter gun and shoot the wall of their "gold mine." They would then sell their claim to some unsuspecting "would be" miner. Many people around the country were swindled by schemes like these. Below – Mrs. Arthur Simpson with her two sons, Frank and Floyd. The view is looking northwest. From the Frances Seely Webb Collection; courtesy Casper College Library.

Below – picture courtesy the Wyoming Field Science Foundation.

EADSVILLE

Below is a copy of a map courtesy Dorothy Putnam. The original map burned in the old Fougstedt cabin that Oly Fougstedt once owned, near the Wa-Wa Lodge.

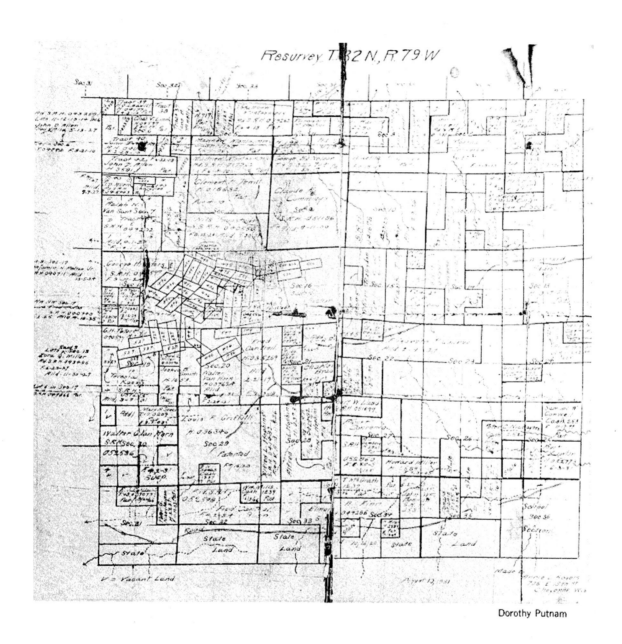

Dorothy Putnam

CASPER MOUNTAIN

Above – A snowy path to the mines in 1905-06. Left – Mr. and Mrs. Cal Cook cabin at Eadsville. Mr. Cook first came to Casper to help install the electric light plant. He later moved his family to the mountain. Photos by Audry Cook McGraugh family. From the True Collection.

EADSVILLE

Left – The remains of Eadsville today. Below – The spring was later encased. The stream runs behind the structure above. Photos by Vaughn S. Cronin.

Right – Bernadine Reed Summer 1996, pointing to a spot where the water is running out of the pond, but is stagnate by the time it gets to the large rock. It is apparently seeping downward. Mrs. Reed had never seen the pond so low.

EADSVILLE

The only known graves at Eadsville are of the Clark children. The Girl Scouts have helped maintain this grave site. Look closely to find the cross markers. Photos by Vaughn S. Cronin.

Watch where you walk. Trees were placed across the mine shaft for safety.

CASPER MOUNTAIN

After the mining activity at Eadsville slowed down the site was used as a Tuberculosis Recuperation Camp. This photo was taken in 1925 of the Tuberculosis Recuperation Camp at Eadsville. Photo by Tom Carrigen; courtesy Casper College Library.

CASPER MOUNTAIN

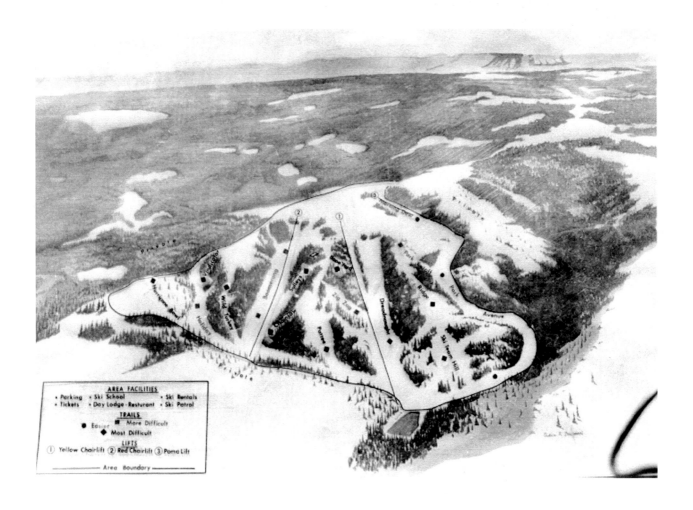

HOGADON SKI AREA

Hogadon ski area is located on top of the mountain at the end of the road after you take the right (west) fork on the main road. I used to work as a lift operator for Dave Furlong in 1974. Instead of the 'Pomma Lift' there was a rope tow, and instead of the two chair lifts, Hogadon had a 'T' Bar. Expert and Boomerang ski runs had many more moguls than they do today. Today the area has 18 groomed trails.

Hogadon (the final 'e' was later dropped) was named after John Charles Hogadone who was the surveyor and mining engineer that laid out the Hogadone Trail up the face of Casper Mountain. The road was first known as the Asbestos Road. The Hogadone Trail did not use the switch-backs that the present road has. Cables were used to help buggies up the steep grade. Today hikers use the old trail east and above Bloody Turnip, which is mostly on private property. The Hogadone Trail should not be confused with the Hogadone Tram Trail that went up the Garden Creek Drainage above Garden Creek Falls. Hogadone also had a claim in the asbestos mine on the mountain.

1958 was the first year that Hogadon was opened. That first year had many traffic accidents. In 1960, a corporation of skiers sold shares of stock. Don Burgess, "a tough marine," was a strong influence in this effort. John Wold was the first president of the corporation.

The City of Casper acquired the ski area in 1975, and it has never made a profit. The city has made several improvements on the ski area over the years in an effort to improve safety and usage of the area. Ski lessons, as well as snowboarding lessons, are available at Hogadon.

Photo by Kim Wrasper Cronin.

Left – Map of the Hogadon Ski Area, by Glenn Bochmann.

CASPER MOUNTAIN

Photos by Vaughn S. Cronin

This is the Pomma Lift going up Morning Dew, the Bunny Slope used by beginning skiers.

Signs along the Pomma Lift aid skiers in safety.

HOGADON SKI AREA

Skiers relax as they come up the main chair lift at Hogadon. Trails like Morning Dew and Dreadnaught were named after mining claims. Pattee was named after Fred Patee, although the spelling was changed on the ski run.

A curious skier watches me take pictures while we are going up the main chairlift at Hogadon. Photo by Vaughn S. Cronin.

CASPER MOUNTAIN

Lift lines are usually short during the week. This was taken the last day of the ski season, 1996. Photo by Vaughn S. Cronin.

Man made snow is used to supplement the snow base. Hogadon likes to open in time for Thanksgiving and closes in March, weather permitting. Photo of 'Bunny' by Vaughn S. Cronin.

HOGADON SKI AREA

Snowboarders on Boomerang at Hogadon, 1996. Photos by Vaughn S. Cronin.

Boomerang had many more moguls in the '60's.

CASPER MOUNTAIN

Below – A summer photo of the main chairlift next to the expert run. Photo by Vaughn S. Cronin.

Next Page – Scenery north of the ski resort. Photo by Vaughn S. Cronin.

CASPER MOUNTAIN

CASPER MOUNTAIN

A snowy day on top of Casper Mountain. This road leads to Muddy Mountain.
Photo by Vaughn S. Cronin.

CASPER MOUNTAIN

ROAD FROM JUNCTION TO MUDDY MOUNTAIN

ROAD FROM JUNCTION TO MUDDY MOUNTAIN

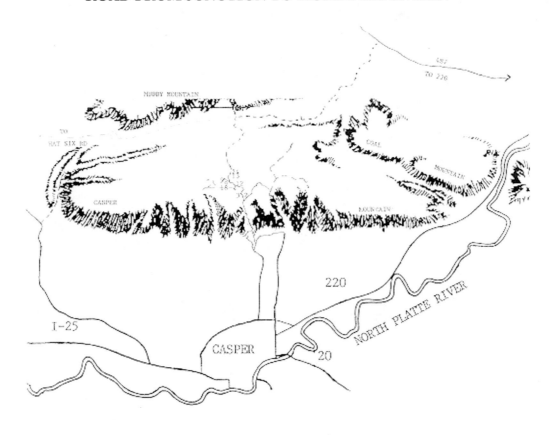

```
    S
E  -+- W
    N
```

* Note that this map is Upside Down from a normal map.

1.	Site of CCC work	0.2 mi.	13.	Bear Trap Meadow	1.2 mi.
2.	Site of Nursery Ski Course	0.2 mi.	14.	Snowmobile Area	1.3 mi.
3.	Park Service Center	0.3 mi.	15.	Deer Haven Park	1.4 mi.
4.	Strube Loop	0.5 mi.	16.	Bear Trap South	1.7 mi.
5.	Information Sign	0.5 mi.	17.	Leaving Bear Trap	1.8 mi.
6.	Lions Camp/old CCC	0.8 mi.	18.	Crimson Dawn Road	2.0 mi.
7.	WYOBA	0.8 mi.	19.	Columbine Circle	2.3 mi.
8.	Upper Nordic Ski Parking Lot	0.8 mi.	20.	Columbine Drive	2.4 mi.
9.	Skunk Hollow Campground	1.0 mi.	21.	El Rancho No Dinoro	2.5 mi.
10.	Lower Nordic Parking	1.0 mi.	22.	Aspen Lane	2.6 mi.
11.	Elkhorn Springs Campground	1.0 mi.	23.	Star Wallow	2.7 mi.
12.	East Entrance Lions Camp	1.0 mi.	24.	Pavement Ends	3.0 mi.

OLD SKI AREAS

About 1/4 mile past the 'Y' in the road to Bear Trap Meadow, to the west, is an old ski area once known as the Nursery Ski Course, 8.3 miles from town. As a high school teenager, my father, Barney Cronin, used to strap his overshoes into his wooden skis and traverse this old trail, in the mid 1930's. I remember in the late '60's using a tow rope to go up the old trail.

At least two buildings have burned to the ground at the edge of this hill. The first burned from a lightning strike and the last building, a restaurant, burned down in 1976.

Another ski area is mentioned in an out of print book called WYOMING, A GUIDE TO ITS HISTORY, HIGHWAYS AND PEOPLE, Oxford University Press, 1941. It tells of a ski area called the Thunder Bolt Ski Course that was 2.5 miles in length that existed 7.4 miles up the face of the mountain, but .3 mile north of the old Asbestos Mine. This run was not packed and had no rope tow. Skiers would have to park one car at the bottom of the run and another car at the top of the run and shuttle each other back and forth. At the base of the ski area stood the Dixie Lodge, 7.4 miles from Casper, at the bottom of the canyon. It was often rented to the Elks Lodge for their activities. The Dixie Lodge was another victim of fire.

Early slopes on the mountain also include: Bumps a Daisy, which is now in the park and used as part of the cross country trails, Miner, that had its own rope tow, named after Lee Miner who was shot during World War II, in Sicily, and Spillway, that has seen racing activity.

Skiing in Wyoming dates back to the 1860's, when Scandinavian linemen used to use skis to maintain the first transcontinental telegraph line. "Others used them to get in and out of snow-locked Wyoming communities," WYOMING, A GUIDE TO ITS HISTORY, HIGHWAYS, AND PEOPLE, 1941.

On Dec. 7, 1941, Rob Robertson and friends were skiing on the mountain. Later that day they would hear the news of the Japanese bombing at Pearl Harbor. We were at war. Photo of Nursery Ski Slope by Ken Ball, courtesy of Ken Ball family.

CASPER MOUNTAIN

Don McManus, Don Burgess, Dwight Osborne, and Dick Perkins were avid skiers, never missing an opportunity. These young men and their friends, Rob Robertson, and Wayne Warren Weaver cut the first slopes around Nursery Ski Slope, Spillway and Miner. Rob remembers Thunderbolt Run built in the 1930's, in the Garden Creek drainage, "It wasn't a trail. It was a disaster!" Photo taken 1941, courtesy Rob Robertson.

Today the hill is mainly used by sleds. Photo by Kim Wrasper Cronin.

BRAILLE TRAIL

In the book <u>A FIELD GUIDE TO THE CASPER MOUNTAIN AREA</u>, 1978, the Braille Trail is chronicled, with a good informative background on this wonderful trail. The Braille Trail is located on the north end of the Strube Loop of the Cross Country Ski Course, also known as the City Park Loop or Skunk Hollow. Elkhorn Creek runs through the site. The trail was created for blind and sighted visitors. Also known as the Lee McCune Braille Trail, it covers 1/3 of a mile and has 37 stations. Signs at each location provide descriptions of rock formations, vegetation and other interesting information. The signs are in Braille and standard printing. The trails have rails or ropes for the blind, as well as sighted visitors, to easily follow for support and balance.

Biology teacher Ed Strube designed the trail in the early 1970's. The plan came from a similar trail found in Colorado. With the help of Field Science students, Dana Van Burgh, the Casper Mountain Lions Club, and other volunteers over a four year period, the trail was completed in 1975.

The U.S. Department of the Interior designated the trail as a component of the National Recreational Trail System in 1976. The Braille Trail was the first in Wyoming to receive this designation.

Photos by Vaughn S. Cronin.

CASPER MOUNTAIN

Nordic Ski Area; Courtesy of the Natrona County Road & Parks Department.

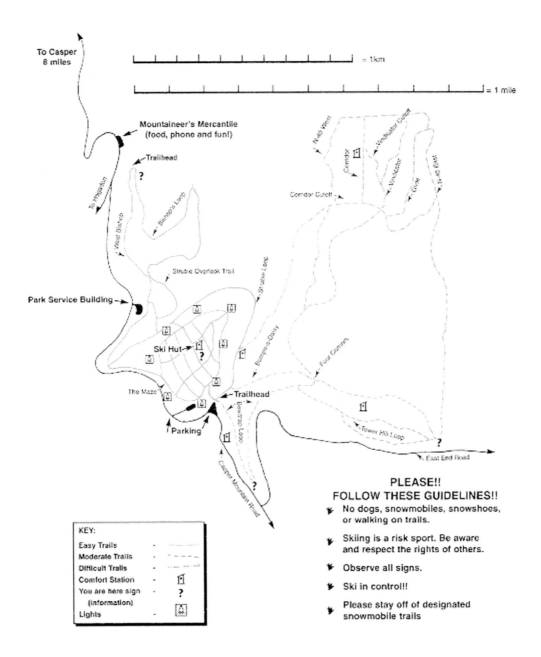

Passes support groomed trails.

Season and Day Passes are available.

CROSS COUNTRY SKIING

Several years ago people would park at the K2 Tower located on the way to Hogadon, and ski in every direction including to Muddy Mountain, Eadsville, and other surrounding areas.

Today, the cross country skiers (Nordic Skiers), have 15 miles of groomed trails just north of Bear Trap Meadow, where the old Strube Loop Road used to be, including the adjoining area. In 1994, lights were added to the trail in "the loop" portion of the ski area, that stay on until 9:00 P.M., Monday through Saturday. Day and season passes are sold at the Mountaineer's Mercantile, and at the Parks Department to maintain the trails.

Lower parking for the Nordic Ski Area. Photo by Kim Wrasper Cronin.

Claire Farrell beats the rush before the Cowboy State Games Feb. 17, 1996. Photo by Vaughn S. Cronin.

CASPER MOUNTAIN

Above – Casper Mountain is known for the 500-acre park. Photo by Vaughn S. Cronin. Below – The author making the night trek at the Nordic Ski Area. Lights were added for night skiing in 1994. Photo by Kim Wrasper Cronin.

CROSS COUNTRY SKIING

In May 1995, heavy snow and wind broke 250,000 trees. Right – Kicho prepares to clear away the devastation. Photo by Vaughn S. Cronin

Left – Note the slash piles left by the destruction and cleanup effort. Photo by Vaughn S. Cronin.

CASPER MOUNTAIN

Below – June 19th, 1996, a new piece of equipment is unloaded to help with the cleanup effort from the trees damaged in 1995. Photo by Vaughn S. Cronin.

Below – Dry Creek Mountain Bike Racers, at Bear Trap Meadow, adjacent to the Cross Country Ski Trails.

CROSS COUNTRY SKIING

In the summer the ski trails are used by the mountain bike racers. Front row, left to right are: #50 Brandon Sweeney, #51 Austin Burgess, #52 Seth Uptain, #85 Mike Diesburg, #54 Andrew Zook, and #306 Dave Chadderon. Also racing: #87 Travis Hunt, #53 Aaron Rodolph, #84 Marty Rozel, #86 Kelly Schramm, #205 Rick Martz, #221 Tom Butler, #304 Woody Motten, #308 Mark Spears, #305 Tom Swanton, #307 Matt Wolf, #5 Pat Bower, #6 Ryan Allison, #9 Dave Brown, and #4 Peter Robinson. The experts rode 31 miles and were led by Pat Bower. Other classes ran 18.6 miles. This photo won a blue ribbon at the Wyoming State Fair at Douglas, in 1996.

Bottom right – #244 Dustin Rude. Photos by Vaughn S. Cronin.

CASPER MOUNTAIN

Below – Members of the Lions Camp prepare for parade day 1996. This is the parade for the Central Wyoming Fair & Rodeo. Left to right – Desirae Amacher, Fred Amacher, Pete Miner, Matt Wales, and Bill Jennings.

THE LIONS CAMP

Also known as the "Blind Camp," or the Stewart Camp, the Lions Camp is across the road from the Cross Country Ski Area, north of Bear Trap Meadow, and adjacent to Camp WYOBA.

Allen H. Stewart was severely injured during World War II. The camp was later named after him. The Civilian Conservation Corps (CCC) was also housed at this location and built some of the earliest structures in the 1930's, like Boyer Hall in 1933 and the barbecue still in use today.

The Allen H. Stewart Camp is a Lions of Wyoming project created to help the visually impaired. It is the only school camp in the state exclusively for blind people. Camp services are free for resident students. Adult sessions as well as separate children's sessions teach many skills that help students cope with their disability. Campers also learn many skills that make them more productive in their personal life. The camp is also used by other groups, like the Association of Retarded Citizens (ARC), that work with the handicapped.

In 1996 the Blind Camp celebrated its 50th anniversary. The camp is really 71 years old, and started out as a milk camp for malnourished children, right after World War I. When World War II started, the young men of the CCC had a new challenge. In 1946 the Casper Lions Club made an agreement with the State Department of Education to use the location for the visually impaired.

Photos by Vaughn S. Cronin.

The Cowboy State Games are held annually. Above – Notice the Lions Club in the background. Picture taken February, 1996.

CASPER MOUNTAIN

Right – Window Rock. A Tom Carrigen photo circa 1925. Courtesy; Wyoming Sate Archives Division of Cultural Resources, Department of Commerce.

A NATURAL BRIDGE LOCATED ON THE MOUNTAIN

A picture of a natural bridge hangs on the wall at the museum at Crimson Dawn. Neal Forsling was told that the natural bridge blew over and was destroyed from wind many years back; that is not true. The natural bridge known as Picture Frame Rock, or Window Rock, stands in Elkhorn Canyon, northeast of the North 40 cross country ski trail near the Mills Spring Camp located on top of the mountain.

Photos by Kevin Anderson taken Oct. 14, 1978.

The view as seen from Picture Frame Rock. Photo by Kevin Anderson.

CASPER MOUNTAIN

Map of snowmobile trails reproduced from the National Forest Service.

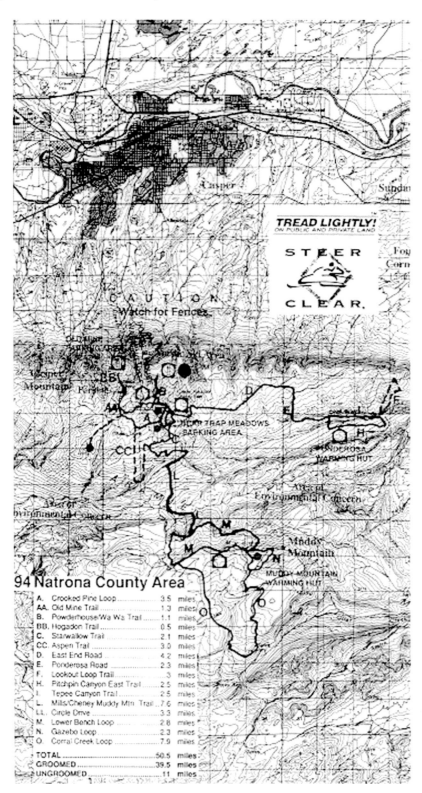

BEAR TRAP MEADOW

Bear Trap Meadow is located on the main road on top of Casper Mountain. It has three picnic shelters that can be reserved with a deposit paid to the Natrona County Road Bridge and Parks Department located in Mills, Wyoming, as well as picnic areas. Snowmobile enthusiasts use Bear Trap as their starting point for their trek over Casper and Muddy Mountains. Snowmobilers have 140 miles of trails in which to ride. Water is available during the summer months.

Photo of Bear Trap by Kim Wrasper Cronin.

Bear Trap in the Winter; photo by Vaughn S. Cronin.

CASPER MOUNTAIN

Bear Trap Meadow in the summertime, photos by Vaughn S. Cronin.

Three shelters on Casper Mountain may be reserved for groups, but may NOT be used for overnight camping (closed 10:00 p.m.-7:00 a.m.). Glass containers are prohibited at all county parks.

BEAR TRAP MEADOW

Three year old Corey Cronin enjoys Bear Trap Meadow. Photos by Vaughn S. Cronin.

CASPER MOUNTAIN

Bear Trap is the site of the Beartrap Summer Festival. Black Rose, above, with Dick Carlson, Hope Kressner and Charlie Hall. Right – Black Rose practices before the show. Below – Paul Hanson mixes the sound. Photos by Vaughn S. Cronin.

BEAR TRAP MEADOW

Justin Gates shows his ability as a stunt rider.

The Army National Guard provided power for the Blue Grass Festival. Photos by Vaughn S. Cronin.

Turtle Creek, Kimmel Rosenstein & Co., and Ric-o-chet also provided music at the festival.

CASPER MOUNTAIN

Maps & signs like these can be seen at Bear Trap along the snowmobile route. Photos by Vaughn S. Cronin.

BEAR TRAP MEADOW

Too much Bluegrass? Glenn Troutman and Tom Cummings "ham it up" at the Beartrap Summer Festival July 21, 1996. The hats were purchased at one of the concession stands set up for the event. Photo by Vaughn S. Cronin.

CASPER MOUNTAIN

Remains of a Powder House on Powder House Hill, near Bear Trap Meadow.

The Powder House was used to store explosives for the building of the Casper Mountain Road. Photos by Vaughn S. Cronin.

HIDDEN CAVERN

In the 1960's, a story came out about a cavern in the Bear Trap Meadow area that extended through to the south side of the mountain. It was said that it was large enough to house the entire population of Casper in the event of a nuclear attack. Story also has it that the entrance near Bear Trap was filled in and there was no more talk about the cavern. This was at the time when people were building bomb shelters in their basements or wherever they could find a space for one, for fear of a nuclear attack.

November 12, 1961 the Casper Star-Tribune had an article with the opening line, "A fallout shelter on Casper Mountain large enough to hold the entire population of Natrona County?" The article went on to say that the cavern system would make a good fallout shelter or tourist attraction. Dick Lisco was commissioned to drill seven water wells on Casper Mountain in an effort to better utilize existing picnic areas. This effort was abandoned when his drill bits would fall into caverns ten to thirty-five feet deep.

During a severe runoff at Bear Trap one year the water was swirling and draining in the middle of the meadow. This was back filled with rocks and seen as a potential hazard to people. A metal grate was emplaced.

In Alfred James Mokler's Book, HISTORY OF NATRONA COUNTY WYOMING, 1923 there is a story called Casper Mountain Cave. In it he describes the following information, "Most people in Casper have heard of a cave in Casper Mountain, which is located about two miles east from Eadsville, at the bottom of a large gulch, which in the earlier days attracted considerable interest, but very few people have ever seen it. Those who have penetrated its innermost recesses describe it as being about six feet wide at the entrance and fifteen feet high, making a gradual decline for about fifty yards, some parts of the walls being 40 feet high. About seventy-five yards from the entrance there is a wall which at first appears to be the end of the cave, but there is a small hole in the floor of the cavern large enough for a man to get through by crawling on his hands and knees. This small cavity extends several yards and then a large room is entered, the walls of which are of white, hard sandstone, and there is much crystal quartz adhering to the roof and sidewalls. The floor of this large room, which extends more than four hundred feet into the mountain side, is covered with large timbers and driftwood, which has been carried in during the melting of the snows in the spring and the heavy rains that prevail in the summer months. There is a hole at the farther end of this room, leading to another cave, but the timber and debris must be cleared away before one can descend, and the decent must be made by a rope. After searching the bottom, which is down about ten feet, in order to go further, you must again crawl on your hands and knees, then you come to another large room at the far end of which is a small aperture, but it is so small that a man cannot go through, and there his investigation must end."

Since the Mokler story, debris from a fire has plugged some of the cave off from exploration. A local cave exploration club, the "Hole in the Wall Grotto," has been trying to restore the cave to its former grandeur. Story has it that at the end of the cave, water from an underground source can be heard along with a cold wind.

CASPER MOUNTAIN

Are these cavern systems one and the same? There is also mention of the Ice Cave in the Ice Canyon. This may be another name for the Casper Mountain Cave.

Other caves and mines are known to exist on the mountain. Never go into a cave, mine or cavern without someone knowing your whereabouts, otherwise it may be a one way trip. Davy Crockett (grandnephew of the famous Davy Crockett) and Bill Robertson were lost in the Casper Mountain cave for 72 hours.

Above – entrance to Casper Mountain. Cave. Three-year-old Corey Cronin, top right, stands at entrance. Bottom – sinkhole at Bear Trap. Both systems may link for water drainage. Bob Adams remembered when a dye test was done at the cave. The colored water reappeared at Jackson Canyon. Photos by V.S. Cronin.

TOWER HILL

Tower Hill stands to the east of Bear Trap Meadow. The red flashing beacons can be seen at night from Casper. It is on the East End Road.

Photo by Kim Wrasper Cronin.

CASPER MOUNTAIN

The towers are owned by private and federal entities. They are used for communication such as television, radio, telephone or encoded messages.

Photos by Vaughn S. Cronin.

EAST END ROAD

The East End Road has been improved over the years. However, a chain was put across the road where it crossed private property and the road was closed. A court case ensued and the property owner won. The closed route of the East End Road takes you down wild one lane switch-backs. I would recommend using a four wheel drive and go very slow if you ever get the opportunity to come down the east end.

One place of note that you can still reach on the East End Road is Crimson Dawn. If you could follow East End Road to the end you would wind up on Hat Six Road through the Hat Six Ranch.

Photos by Vaughn S. Cronin.

The famous chained road. This has been a conversational episode in the history of Casper Mountain.

Right – The shelter at Ponderosa Park. In the winter Pitchpin & Tipi Trails are groomed for snow-mobiles. Teepee poles were once found in Tipi Canyon. Indians once hunted here. Teepee can be correctly spelled Tepee, teepee, or tipi.

CASPER MOUNTAIN

Photo by Vaughn S. Cronin.

CRIMSON DAWN

Today, Crimson Dawn is best known for its Midsummer's Eve celebration that started in 1929, done on June 21st each year. "Midsummer's Eve is a celebration of nature by those who love her" Neal Forsling, CRIMSON DAWN, THE STORY OF THE CASPER MOUNTAIN WITCHES, 1980. The celebration is done on a summer evening, on the longest day of the year. Stories of witches and fanciful creatures are told at each station that has been established for each of the individual witches. At the end of the guided tour a bon fire is set on the south end of the red butte.

Participants are told to make a wish and pick up a handful of the red dirt. They are told to throw it into the fire saying "red earth burn." Not everyone will get their wish, but some lucky person will "have a pleasant surprise."

Spanish folklore, mythology and Norse cultures have celebrated Midsummer's Eve for quite some time. Mrs. Neal Forsling brought this tradition to Casper Mountain for us to enjoy.

Crimson Dawn can be reached by taking Tower Hill Road to East End Road, or by turning left off onto the Crimson Dawn Road, past Bear Trap Meadow. This road is marked.

A museum, once Neal's homestead, is accessible with the history and many exciting stories from the Forsling family. Mrs. Neal Forsling wrote a book called CRIMSON DAWN, THE STORY OF THE CASPER MOUNTAIN WITCHES, The Glenwood Corporation, 1980, that can be purchased at the museum. "Witch Jade" was to be the original title of the book.

Painting is titled: "Vista, The Paths, Bates Hole, and Pedros"

Neal is describing her painting titled "Vista, the Paths, Bates Hole, and Pedros." From the Frances Seely Webb Collection; courtesy Casper College Library.

Neal Forsling, friend of Harry and Bess Truman, homesteaded 640 acres, painted in oils, and created the shrines that are celebrated at Midsummer's Eve. In 1941 her husband, Jim Forsling, skied down the mountain for supplies. He did not return. His frozen body was found a short distance from the warmth of the cabin. Jim died March 3, 1942.

CASPER MOUNTAIN

On her 84th birthday (1973) Neal Forsling gave 96 acres of the Red Butte area to the Natrona County Park Department. This earned her an award from the Department of the Interior. The Parks Department has made improvements to the trails as well as preserving Neal's cabin as a museum.

Both Jim and Neal (Elizabeth) are interred on the red butte near the Forsling cabin along with their daughter, Jean Loomis. Jean had retired as a Captain in the Air Force.

Eleanor Carrigen is the curator at Crimson Dawn today. This is a photo of her in her home in 1996. Photo by Vaughn S. Cronin.

Neal started her stories as a means of entertainment for her children and later the community. It was said that an actual coven of witches practiced on the mountain; this is untrue. A satanic group tried unsuccessfully to align themselves with Crimson Dawn. The group sacrificed chickens and other animals in their night ceremonies. Although these practices were not done at Crimson Dawn, the reputation although untrue, did hurt. Neal's stories were for entertainment, not for satanic practices.

CRIMSON DAWN

Below, pictures of Forsling homestead, now known as the Crimson Dawn Museum. Photos by Vaughn S. Cronin.

CASPER MOUNTAIN

An eerie fog settles into the background for Midsummer's Eve 1996. Neal got the idea for Midsummer's Eve from Shakespeare's A Midsummer Night's Dream. Photo by Bob Bondurant.

Inside the museum; Photo by Bob Bondurant.

CRIMSON DAWN

Above, Eleanor Carrigen, the curator at the Crimson Dawn Museum, remembers when Crimson Dawn was best known as Neal's new homestead in 1929. It was formerly the Sanford place.

Another look inside of the museum. Photos by Bob Bondurant.

CASPER MOUNTAIN

Left, Neal's daughter, Mary Martin, with Eleanor Carrigen at the museum.

Right, a peek into another part of the museum. Photos by Bob Bondurant.

Rebecca Weaver Hunt narrating at Midsummer's Eve 1997 Photo by Vaughn S. Cronin

Katie Drinks some hot cocoa after the tour. Photo by Bob Bondurant.

CASPER MOUNTAIN

Shrine of the Good Brother with Neal's grandson Dave Martin. Photos courtesy Bob Bondurant.

Branch, Root and Twig (Alex Martin Paul Bowron, and Chris Weaver).

Shawn the Leprechaun (Keith James).

CRIMSON DAWN

Elizabeth Paxton was a friend of Bess Wallace at Independence, Missouri. Later, after Elizabeth started going by Neal, and had married Jim Forsling, her old friend Bess came to Wyoming to visit with her husband Harry Truman. The press lost track of the famous presidential couple, only to find out later that they were being entertained by Neal Forsling.

The Woodland Theater at Crimson Dawn has been a favorite spot during the Midsummer's Eve Celebration as well as for many weddings. Split log benches, and a stage make the theater a favorite for many to enjoy.

Early one morning, when Neal first got the homestead, the sky and earth were a crimson red. "What a beautiful crimson dawn," Neal thought. From that day on, the area was known as Crimson Dawn.

From Crimson Dawn, at or near the southeast property boundary is the Hazelton Trail. This trail makes an abrupt turn and becomes the Sawmill Trail which leads into Ponderosa Park. Ponderosa Park is noted for Pitchpin and Tipi trails. Steve Lund heard of a teepee ring east of Crimson Dawn. He did not find it, although he did find other Indian artifacts on and around the mountain.

Photos page 182; top left – The Topaz Witch (Debbie Weakland), top right – The Lavender Witch (Dyann Durst) with Vermillion (John Scott), Below left – The Phantom Woodchopper (Don Henry) and Bottom Right – The Star Witch (Phyllis Cotherman). Photos courtesy of Bob Bondurant.

Photos page 183 top – The Emerald Witch (Susan Glasgow), middle – Undine the Homesick Seawitch (JoAnne Ahrndt), below – The Black Witch (Kerry Downey).

CASPER MOUNTAIN

CRIMSON DAWN

CASPER MOUNTAIN

Above, – Midsummer's Eve, 1993. Spectators are told to make a wish, grab a handful of dirt, and yell "red earth burn" as they throw it into the air. Legend says that "One lucky person will be happily surprised." Photo by Bruce Nichols.

Below – the flag waves on the Red Butte, 1996. Photo by Vaughn S. Cronin. The Woodland Theater at Crimson Dawn is another attraction for visitors.

CRIMSON DAWN

Right, The Dog Graveyard. Warren Weaver created this art form as well as the Tin Owl. The dog is patterned after a dog Wayne Weaver, a WWII soldier of the 10th Mountain Div., brought home. It was a Portier Carrier of German and Japanese origin known as a Sherps. These dogs were very intelligent. Photo by Vaughn S. Cronin.

Below, left to right, the grave sites of Jean Loomis (daughter of Neal), Elizabeth (Neal) Forsling, and Jim Forsling. Photo by Vaughn S. Cronin.

CASPER MOUNTAIN

Even summer evenings on the mountain are cold. Wear warm clothing. Photos by Bob Bondurant.

The crowd warms up after their journey with hot cocoa.

OUTER DRIVE ROAD TO HIGHWAY 220

An aerial photo of Casper and Muddy Mountains. Photo by Dana Van Burgh, with pilots Judy Logue and Linda Wackwitz; Courtesy; the Wyoming Field Science Foundation.

CASPER MOUNTAIN

Photos by Vaughn S. Cronin.

OUTER DRIVE INTERSECTION TO HAT SIX ROAD

It is possible to take the road between Casper and Muddy Mountains east to Hat Six Road. A four-wheel drive truck is recommended even on a dry day. Expect a well-rutted road. You will have to open gates along the route. Below are photos of that journey. Notice the mountain bike in the back of the pickup. The road ends near mile marker 9 on Hat Six Road. Photos by Vaughn S. Cronin.

CASPER MOUNTAIN

The road swerves to avoid The Jenkins Trench, which runs through the center of this picture. Named after Carl Jenkins, a geologist who had a cabin near Window Rock, it is a natural feature. Keep looking in your rear view mirror to find this spot. Photos by Vaughn S. Cronin.

This area is below the Jenkins Trench looking at Muddy Mountain. The red color is due to oxidation or rust of the iron minerals present in an old sea bed, "where the water was shallow," <u>A FIELD GUIDE TO THE CASPER MOUNTAIN AREA</u>, The Wyoming Field Science Foundation, Casper, WY, 1978. Photos by Vaughn S. Cronin.

OUTER DRIVE ROAD TO HIGHWAY 220

The Fredericks' cabin was built by John and Zelta Fredericks in 1911. Although the cabin was built on the north side of the road, their barn stood on the south side of the road until 1978. In the 1920's Mrs. Gladys Huffard maintained the Freeland Post Office in the old Fredericks' cabin. The Freeland District Post Office and Railroad Station were named after Bill Freeland, a rancher in Bates Hole.

Photo by Vaughn S. Cronin.

Photo by Kim Wrasper Cronin.

CASPER MOUNTAIN

WEST END

MAP OF WEST END

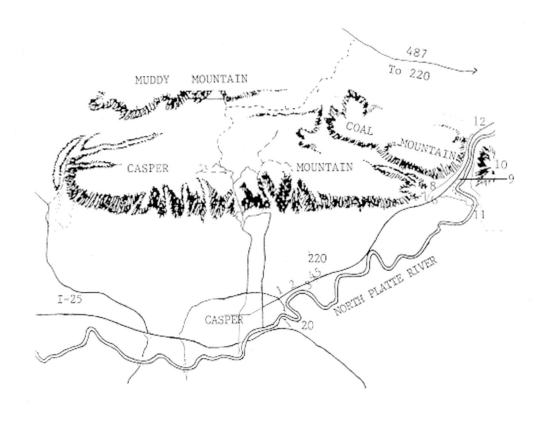

*Note that this is map is upside down from a normal map.

1. Wolf Creek	.4 mi.	7. Goose Egg Gallery	7.5 mi.
2. Squaw Creek	.6 mi.	8. Jackson Canyon	8.0 mi.
3. Battle of Red Butte Marker	3.0 mi.	9. Astoria Cabin Marker	9.7 mi.
4. Tennessee Walkers	3.3 mi.	10. Red Butte	10.2 mi.
5. Platte River Fly Shop	3.7 mi.	11. Goose Egg Ranch	10.1 mi.
6. Goose Egg Restaurant	7.5 mi.	12. Coal Mountain	12.1 mi.

WOLF CREEK

Wolf Creek Road starts near mile marker 113 on highway 220, just south of Wyoming Blvd. on CY Avenue, heading southeast. It is a short trip to a large sign over the top of the road marking the Asbell Ranch. Bill and Sue Asbell own the ranch with the No Trespassing sign.

Mr. Asbell had a large construction company that did a lot of roadwork in the state, like the Casper Mountain road in 1962, as well as work in neighboring states. He is also a noted big game hunter who has a collection to rival the Werner Wildlife Museum. His collection of big game trophies spans the globe.

Their ranch was originally the Price Dairy, homesteaded in the 1880's, that the Asbell couple purchased in 1963. At one time Casper had thirty dairies, now there are none. They also owned the land that is now the Wolf Creek Subdivision southeast of the CY Buttrey store. Ray Whitaker owned the land where the subdivision now sits.

Photo by Vaughn S. Cronin.

Fred Coates remembers the oldest trail going up Wolf Creek. He also remembers when "you could find teepee rings everywhere." Mary Price also told of "teepee rings up by the spring." Today little sign of these teepee rings remains.

CASPER MOUNTAIN

Photos by Vaughn S. Cronin.

Bill and Sue Asbell in 1966. Photo by Bob Dorn; courtesy the Asbell collection.

CASPER MOUNTAIN

Above and left – Pinnacles on the north face of the mountain near Squaw Creek. Photos by Vaughn S. Cronin.

Right – Look above fence post #4 for Hogadon Ski Area. Right of telephone pole is Fox Farm Peak.

SQUAW CREEK

The Squaw Creek Road is just west of Casper off of Highway 220. Legend has it that the creek was named by an old pioneer who saw Indian Squaws doing their wash at the creek.

Steve Lund in his narrative THE ARCHAEOLOGICAL RECORD OF CASPER MOUNTAIN, 1976, writes of artifacts found in the area, "Section 14 of Range 80 W., Township 32 N., contains the largest number of sites yet encountered by the writer on Casper Mountain." The sites showed considerable amounts of tool manufacturing made of quartzite. The tools dated back to the Middle Prehistoric Period. The largest find is at the headwaters of Squaw Creek on the face of the mountain. This has been a popular spot for artifact collectors for many years.

At the end of the present-day traveled road, stands the old Galles Slaughterhouse. Walt Galles leased the building out to Dave Lenhart, Walt Houston and Harold Houston. It was known as the Squaw Creek Packing Plant. The Beef from the slaughterhouse was cheaper and had larger cuts than the other local competitors could offer.

Walt Galles had the ranch house and the Galles Silver Fox Farm from 1927 to 1947. Walt spent several thousand dollars in 1939 for a silver fox because of the rarity of the animal and the demand for them. The next page shows the ranch house, observation tower, and most of the pens. Eventually more pens were built by the barn for a total of 100 cages, with two animals in each cage. Also near the barn were some tepee rings that no longer exist. The slaughterhouse would be to the extreme right side of the picture. Photo courtesy the Don Galles collection.

Don Galles remembers a bootleggers cave that he and Paul Jacques used to visit. Paul would encase potatoes in mud and bake them in this cave. "It was like heaven," Don recalls. Fred Coates remembers two stills in the area that were both destroyed by grass fires.

After Walt Galles sold the property a counterfeiting ring was discovered near the slaughter house in 1956. The counterfeiter made $20 bills. The tale goes that he got caught when he sent two prostitutes to Montana "to make change." They bungled the scheme and confessed.

The slaughterhouse as it looks today. Photo by Vaughn S. Cronin.

SQUAW CREEK

In the summer of 1943 (pictured) is a litter of nine fox pups, seven were platinum and two were silver. Front row – George Humphreys, Don Galles. Back row – Bob Pennington, Walter Galles, Paul Jacques, Doris Jacques, Marge Mathews and Gladys Galles. Photo courtesy of the Galles collection.

CASPER MOUNTAIN

Heading west along Highway 220 to the left is the Pursel Ranch, home of the Tennessee Walkers. Whitey Pursel took pride in his ranch. He was also involved in roadwork and irrigation projects around the area. The barn was moved from the CY Ranch.

Photos by Vaughn S. Cronin.

In the 1960's beautiful horses would graze in this pasture.

CASPER MOUNTAIN

The Platte River Fly Shop is easily seen on the south (left) as you traverse Highway 220. It is noted for float trips as well as guided walking trips and many other services. Timberline Sporting Goods, Bullwinkle's Bait & Tackle and other stores along the route have helped me immensely with hunting and fishing gear over the years. I wouldn't want to leave them out.

Although not along this route, The Ugly Bug Fly Shop on Midwest Avenue can also fill your fly fishing needs. Rob Robinder, taught classes on fly tying and fishing at Casper College. Other great places not along the route include Dean's Sporting Goods, Coast to Coast, Country General, Bi-Rite, and others. See the phone book for specifics.

Photo by Vaughn S. Cronin.

This historic building was actually two school houses. The first (left) school house was built at Wolton (later renamed Hiland) in 1907. The birdseye maple floor was added in 1910. The second school was built at Arminto around 1913. The Wolton school was moved to Arminto and joined to the second schoolhouse.

These school houses were later moved to this present site.

CASPER MOUNTAIN

Picture of the Red Buttes as seen along the Platte River & Highway 220.

Oil rigs blaze on the set of the Hellfighters, shot near Red Butte, 1968. Photo by Vaughn S. Cronin.

I was lucky enough to get John Wayne's autograph when he stayed at the Holiday Inn at Casper, 1968.

RED BUTTE

In 1968 John Wayne came to Casper to make the movie "The Hellfighters" near Red Butte and Highway 220 along the North Platte River. Our family piled into the 1967 Dodge and I shot the pictures of the oil rigs burning. They had a total of five oil rigs on the set.

John Wayne and the director, John Houston, stayed at the Holiday Inn at Casper. I had the privilege of meeting them and getting John Wayne's autograph. Later according to the Casper Star-Tribune, April 26, 1996 "Wayne was moved into a house at an undisclosed location – where rumor had it, he brought his own butler and cook to live with him. "The community got involved in the movie by renting out jeeps and playing extras in the movie. Extras were paid $1.60 an hour for their parts.

Wayne played the part of Red Adair, an actual firefighter. Katherine Ross played the part of his daughter, with Vera Miles cast as the wife. Bruce Cabot was the co-star.

John Wayne & Katherine Ross on the movie set "The Hellfighters" May 1968, Star-Tribune file.

JACKSON CANYON

Jackson Canyon is located on the west end of Casper Mountain, east of the Goose Egg Road, just off of highway 220. It was named after the famous photographer William H. Jackson who discovered it in 1870. Jackson was a member of the Hayden Expedition that traveled up the valley of the North Platte River. The Hayden Expedition conducted scientific study in the area.

Indian artifacts have been found on the upper rim of the canyon and surrounding area. The Goose Egg Restaurant is located north of the canyon. It has been a favorite eatery for many years. It is named after the Goose Egg Ranch once located at Bessemer, Wyoming. Owen Wister made the ranch famous in his book, THE VIRGINIAN.

The Goose Egg art gallery across the road from the Goose Egg Restaurant is another great stopping place.

Below is an aerial view of the west end of Casper Mountain. Photo by Dana Van Burgh, with pilots Judy Logue and Linda Wackwitz; courtesy the Wyoming Field Science Foundation.

CASPER MOUNTAIN

Bob Adams remembered a dye test done at Casper Mountain Cave. The colored dye reappeared at Jackson Canyon.

Above – Jackson Canyon photo by Vaughn S. Cronin.
Below – Jackson Canyon 1995 photo courtesy Pierre Nichols.

JACKSON CANYON

Above is a picture of the Goose Egg Restaurant. Below is the Goose Egg Gallery. Photos by Vaughn S. Cronin.

CASPER MOUNTAIN

The Hayden party surveyed much of Wyoming including Jackson Canyon, named after the photographer. Below is an 1871 photograph with H.W. Elliot (sketch artist), Dr. C. S. Turnbull; unidentified, and Dr. F.V. Hayden. Courtesy American Heritage Center, University of Wyoming.

Photographs taken by William H. Jackson, while as a member of the Hayden Expedition, later convinced Congress that Yellowstone should become a national park. Gold was discovered near the west end of the mountain on March 6, 1891 by J.E. Daine and G. E. Butler. Although an experienced miner was involved, the claim was soon found to be of very low quality.

Next page, photos of Jackson Canyon by Vaughn S. Cronin.

JACKSON CANYON

Left – the countryside as you walk to the south rim of Jackson Canyon. Photos by Vaughn S. Cronin.

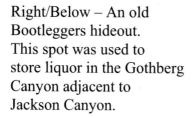

Right/Below – An old Bootleggers hideout. This spot was used to store liquor in the Gothberg Canyon adjacent to Jackson Canyon.

CASPER MOUNTAIN

Photos by Vaughn S. Cronin.

FIRST CABIN IN WYOMING

The first cabin built in Wyoming was at the base of Casper and Muddy Mountains, on the North Platte River. John Jacob Astor commissioned the first expedition across Wyoming led by Robert Stuart. Astor needed an overland route to his fur trading post Astoria, located on the Columbia River. Robert Stuart, an American explorer born in Scotland, and his band of fur traders built the cabin on November 2, 1812 near Bessemer Bend, in what was later to be known as Wyoming. The cabin was eight feet by eighteen feet with a fire in the middle in the Indian fashion. The sides were six feet high, and the hole was covered with buffalo skins for shelter. Buffalo were plentiful in the area at that time.

These fur traders shortened the route that Lewis and Clark had taken by being the first white men known to go through South Pass, Sweetwater River, and the North Platte River. The North Platte River got its French name in 1739, meaning broad and shallow. The party traveled over what was to become the Overland and the Oregon Trails. The Oregon Trail covered over 2,000 miles from Independence, Missouri, to the Columbia River. More than 300,000 people traveled it from 1840-1869. Although Stuart's party didn't know it, they crossed the continental divide and passed by Independence Rock. Members of the group included: Robert Stuart, Ben Jones, Robert McClellan, John Day, Robert Crooks, Andri Vallar, and Francis LeClerc.

There were cottonwoods and willows for firewood and building materials. A.J. Mokler's Book <u>HISTORY OF NATRONA COUNTY WYOMING</u>, 1923 tells the story of the Astoria Cabin in detail. At what is now known as Fremont Canyon, "Stuart gave, from the color of the impending rocks, the name of The Fiery Narrows," not to be confused with "The Narrows" or "The Bessemer Narrows" which is the area nearby the cabin site.

Twenty-three Arapahoe Indians visited the leery fur trappers. The Indians left without harming them. But the Stuart party left after the Indian visit and moved their camp near the present site of Torrington, Wyoming or Gering, Nebraska.

If you park at this marker and look northwest; just above the water tower at the Speas Fish Hatchery, you will see the "Rock Wall" location on the low ridge. Photo by Vaughn S. Cronin.

CASPER MOUNTAIN

T. A. Larson's book <u>HISTORY OF WYOMING</u>, 1965, states that historians disagree as to the actual location of the cabin. Two areas are commonly discussed as the actual site. Stuart was noted for walking two miles and calling it three miles. The Stuart Journal has had to be adjusted in this manner to make the account by Stuart and the physical evidence agree.

Ed Gothberg first shed some light on the existence of one of the possible sites of the Astoria Cabin. His grandfather, Martin J. Gothberg, worked at the Goose Egg Ranch in 1880. One day he stumbled onto the remains of the old Stuart Cabin (rock wall site) near what is now the Speas Fish Hatchery. Most of the three-foot tall walls were still standing. He asked the owner of the Goose Egg, Mr. Searight, what that was. The Searight brothers started the Goose Egg Ranch, on the Poison Spider Creek, in 1877 when they trailed in 27,000 head of cattle from Texas. Mr. Searight, who knew the area very well around his ranch stated very matter of factly "It was the old Stuart Cabin." That came from an article by Norman D. Weis in the 55th Annual Wyoming Edition of the <u>Casper Star Tribune</u>, Feb 18, 1973. M. J. Gothberg had a reputation for his honesty.

Confusion about the exact location is compounded by the lack of detail in early maps, and what is now called Goose Egg Creek (also known as Goose Egg Spring, Speas Spring, Red Springs Creek, and Poison Springs Creek, and Poison Spring) being left off of some of the maps. This may have been confused with Poison Spider Creek, which is also near Bessemer Bend. Norman D. Weis tracked down the history and location of the original Stuart diary, a task that took four years to accomplish, and subsequent later writings of the trip by Stuart, and concludes that the rock wall site is indeed the correct location.

Martin J. Gothberg and Dan Speas reported seeing the Stuart Cabin when the walls were about three feet high. Rotten buffalo hides were found in the ruins. Pictured next page is Jack Romanek at the site near the Speas Fish Hatchery, photo courtesy Norman D. Weis. Critics claim that the rock structure was too small to have housed the number of people in the party. Those who disclaim this as the actual site say this was used by early hunters as a "hunting blind," and not the original Astoria Cabin, although it is unclear who built it.

An historian named Rollins, who had not heard of the rock wall site, went downstream from Poison Spider Creek, and found tree stumps that could have been used for the Stuart cabin (instead of rock) at that location, although no remains of the cabin were found. The wandering North Platte River could have flooded and carried important clues away. This is the most widely accepted spot, by historians, as the site of the Astoria Cabin. Historian Chuck Morrison also claimed to have found tree stumps below Poison Spider Creek, perhaps the same ones. In any instance, the error of margin is a difference of a few miles between the rock wall site, and the Poison Spider Creek site, for this historic cabin.

FIRST CABIN IN WYOMING

Jack Romanek looks over the rock wall site of Stuart's Astoria Cabin. Photo courtesy Norman D. Weis.

CASPER MOUNTAIN

The town of Bessemer was built ¼ mile west of the Goose Egg Ranch. It was known as the "Queen City of the Plains." Bessemer Bend was known for its fertile valley. The town was named after Sir Henry Bessemer, who invented a process of making steel from cast iron. Judge Joseph M. Carey later bought the ranch just before the harsh winter of 1886.

Bessemer lost an election for the county seat after it was reported that local residents had stuffed the ballots. Soon after that, the bridge was seized for back taxes and the town failed shortly after. Almost no sign of the town is visible today.

"Searight brothers trailed in 27,000 head of cattle from Texas and established ranch on Poison Spider Creek in 1877. Cowboys found a nest of wild goose eggs and brought them back to the cook; gave owners an idea for a brand and a ranch name." Mae Urbanek, WYOMING PLACE NAMES, Johnson Publishing Co., Boulder, CO, 1967. The book goes on to say "Cowboys quarried stone on Casper Mountain and built a two story stone house." The rest of the building material came from Cheyenne, Wyoming. A victim of vandalism and neglect, the house was demolished in 1951. Below – Tom Carrigen photo of the Goose Egg Ranch House from the Wyoming State Archives Division of Cultural Resources, Department of Commerce.

COAL MOUNTAIN ROAD

Following highway 220, you will pass Coal Mountain Road. It is a beautiful spot although people have been dumping trash out there and ruining the area.

A lone cross blends in with the prairie behind the Coal Mountain Road sign. Below is another view of the lone cross by Coal Mountain Road. Crosses indicate spots along the highway where wrecks have occurred resulting in highway fatalities. In 1994 the news reported that Highway 220 between Casper and Rawlins was the "bloodiest stretch of highway in the state." Photos by Vaughn S. Cronin.

BIBLIOGRAPHY

Bryant B. Brooks, THE MEMOIRS OF BRYANT B. BROOKS, The Arthur Clark Company, 1939

Ed Bille, WYOMING, A PICTORIAL OVERVIEW, Mountain States Lithographing, 1989

Lavinia Dobler, I DIDN'T KNOW THAT ABOUT WYOMING!, Greybull, Wolverine Gallery, 1990

Neal Forsling, CRIMSON DAWN, THE STORY OF THE CASPER MOUNTAIN WITCHES, The Glenwood Corporation, 1980

Irving Garbutt, and Chuck Morrison, HISTORY OF CASPER AND NATRONA COUNTY, WYOMING, 1889-1989, Dallas, Texas, Curtis Media, 1990

Kathleen Hemry, KATHLEEN'S BOOK, AN ALBUM OF EARLY PIONEER WYOMING IN WORD AND PICTURE, Mountain States Lithographing, 1989

Jim Keith, BLACK HELICOPTERS OVER AMERICA, STRIKEFORCE FOR THE NEW WORLD ORDER, IllumiNet Press, 1994

Edna Gorrell Kukura and Susan Niethammer True, CASPER, A PICTORIAL HISTORY, The Donning Company Publishers, 1986

T.A. Larson, HISTORY OF WYOMING, University of Nebraska Press, 1978

Steve Lund, ARCHAEOLOGICAL RECORD OF CASPER MOUNTAIN, 1976

Steve Lund, RECORDS IN STONE AND BONE, 1975

Alfred J. Mokler, HISTORY OF NATRONA COUNTY, R.R. Donnelley & Sons Company, The Lakeside Press, 1923

Patrick Parmenter, Kelly Moore, Arno U. Ilgner, HIGH PLAINS CLIMBS, A GUIDE TO THE CASPER MOUNTAIN AREA, 1983

Mary Lou Pence and Lola M. Homsher, THE GHOST TOWNS OF WYOMING, Hastings House Publishers, New York, 1956

Art Randall, JOHNNY ARNOLD, 1986

Art Randall, CASPER "OLD TOWN" AND FREMONT, ELKHORN, AND MISSOURI VALLEY RAILROAD, Atlas Reproduction, 1991

BIBLIOGRAPHY

Art Randall, COPPEROPOLIS, A GHOST TOWN ON TOP OF CASPER MOUNTAIN, Private Printing, 1992

Art Randall, EADSVILLE, THE TOWN THAT WAS, Private Printing, 1980

Mae Urbanek, WYOMING PLACE NAMES, Johnson Publishing Co, Boulder CO, 1967

Wyoming Field Science Foundation, A FIELD GUIDE TO THE CASPER MOUNTAIN AREA, The Wyoming Field Science Foundation Casper, Wyoming 1978

Owen Wister, THE VIRGINIAN, Washington Square Press, published by Maxmillion, 1902

Workers of the Writers Program, WYOMING A GUIDE TO IT'S HISTORY, HIGHWAYS, AND PEOPLE, Oxford University Press, 1941

Casper Zonta Club, CASPER CHRONICLES, 1964

Newspapers:

Casper Star-Tribune, Nov 12, 1961, Jul 29, 1967, Feb 18, 1973, 55th Annual Wyoming Edition, Feb 2, 1996, Apr 28, 1996

Denver Post, Nov 25, 1956

Natrona County Tribune, May 13, 1908

Rock Springs Daily Rocket Miner, Aug 14, 1996

Wyoming Derrick, 12 Nov 1891, 17 Dec 1891

Periodicals:

Casper Magazine, March/April 1983

Brochure:

Casper Mountain's Nordic Ski Area, Natrona County Roads, Bridges & Parks Department

Internet

http://freeamerica.com/gvcon2html by Harry V. Martin - Black Helicopters

INTERVIEWS

Alvarez, Edward T. Feb 14, 1996, in person

Asbell, Bill & Sue Jul 22, 1996, in person

Ball, Dave Feb 20, 1996, in person

Berst, Bruce Jul 7, 1996, in person

Bourbon, Kent Dec 31, 1995, in person

Brown, Ben Jul 10, 1996, per telephone

Carrigen, Eleanor Feb 22, 1996, in person

Cartier, Ada Cottman Feb 20, 1996, per telephone

Cronin, Barney Jan 31, 1996, in person

Doherty, Jim Feb 2, 1996, in person

Edgerly, Len July 23, 1996, in person

Erbert, Ray Apr 2, 1996, in person

Garbutt, Irving Mar 26, per telephone

Galles, Don Aug 24, 1996, in person

Gillingham, Blaine B. Jan 22, 1996 in person

Gothberg, Angela Mar 26, 1996, per telephone

Haines, Bill Jr. – Mar 26, per telephone

Hemry, Kathleen Nov 16, 1996, in person

Hopkins, Ruth Joy Simpson Feb 20, 1996, per telephone

Kading, Joye Aug 29, 1996, per telephone

Lam, Dean Jun 27, 1996 in person

INTERVIEWS

Lathrop, Homer and Virginia, Feb 20, 1996, per telephone

McCleary, Bryant Feb 26, 1996, per telephone

McGraugh, Audry, Cook Dec 18, 1998, in person

Morrison, Mary Lou Feb 12, 1996, in person

Mosteller, Charlie May 12, 1996, in person

Nichols, Pierre Feb 17 1996, in person

O'Quinn, Donna Jul 18, 1996 in person

Price, Mary Aug 24, 1996 per telephone

Randall, Art Apr 24, 1996, per telephone

Reed, Bernadine Mar 30, 1996, in person

Robertson, Rob Feb 20, 1996, per telephone

Sutphin, Kevin Dec 31, 1995, in person

True, Susan Apr 19, 1996, in person

Trumbull, Shelly Jan 17, 1997, in person

Van Burgh, Dana Sep 18, 1996, in person

Ward, Lonnie Feb 3, 1996, in person

Weaver, Sam Aug 25, 1996 in person

Weaver, Warren (Buck) Jul 18, 1996, in person

Weis, Norman D. May 19, 1996, in person

Wenger, Curt & Kathy Mar 25, 1996, in person

Wrasper, Harry Feb 16, 1996, in person

Zerby, Dave Aug 20, 1996, in person

GLOSSARY

Archaeological: Historic or prehistoric people and their artifacts.

Alpine Skiing: Elevated mountain skiing, or Downhill Skiing.

Amethyst: Purple or violet quartz gemstone

Artifacts: Objects that were man made or altered by man.

Asbestos: A mineral used in making fireproof items.

Assay: Analysis of an ore to determine the quality.

ATV: All Terrain Vehicle.

Beacon: A guiding or warning signal in an elevated position.

Bomb Shelter: An enforced area usually underground, to protect victims from a nuclear attack.

Braille: A combination of raised dots that are read by touch.

Butte: An isolated hill or mountain, usually having a flat top, rising abruptly above the surrounding land.

Cave: A hollow spot in the earth.

Cavern: An underground cave.

Chair Lift: A ski lift that carries people in a chair up the ski run.

Choppers: Helicopters

Fault: A break or fracture in the continuity of a body of rock or a vein with dislocation along the plane of fracture.

Hang Glider: A glider that the pilot hangs from, nothing more than the wings and controls.

Gravity: Sinking or Falling

Hatchery: A place for hatching fish eggs, and raising fish to release in the wild.

GLOSSARY

Hermit: A person living in seclusion.

Hunting Blind: Hiding place for hunter that blends in with surrounding area.

Governor: An executive head of state in the U.S.

Mandrel: A spindle that a saw rotates on.

Mercantile: A place of trade or commerce, pertains to merchants.

Mine: Excavation made in the earth for the purpose of extracting ore, or other precious stones.

Moguls: Bumps or mounds of hard snow on a ski trail.

Nordic Skiing: Another name for Cross Country Skiing.

Norse: Belonging to, or pertaining to Norway, or to ancient Scandinavia.

Pegmatite: An intertwine of quartz, and feldspar.

Reservation: A piece of property set aside by the U.S. Government for Indian tribes.

Revenuer: A U.S. agent of the Department of the Treasury whose job it is to discover and destroy illegal liquor stills, as well as to arrest the owners.

Rope Tow: A rope used to pull a skier up a ski course.

Salting: Using a scatter gun or other method to fraudulently stick gold or other precious ore into a mine to fool an unsuspecting buyer.

Sawmill: A place in which timber is sawed into planks or boards; lumber mill.

Schooner: A sailing vessel with masts and sails.

Slash Piles: The debris of trees stacked in a forested area.

Scatter Gun: Shotgun; sometimes loaded with rock salt or pebbles.

Snow Maker: A machine at a ski area for the purpose of making snow for skiers.

GLOSSARY

Stamp Mill: Mill or machine in which ore is crushed into powder by heavy stampers.

Streetcar: A trolley propelled electrically from an overhead wire, following a set of tracks.

Switch-back: A road in a mountainous area, having many hairpin curves.

"T" Bar: A ski lift that pulled two people up per lift, up a ski run.

Tailings: Refuse remaining after mining.

Tennessee Walkers: A breed of saddle horses bred from Standardbred and Morgan Horses.

Teepee: Also correctly spelled Tepee or tipi, these were the forerunner to the modern day tent. Constructed in a cone shape from animal hides stretched over small tree trunks cut as lodge poles.

Trolley Car: A streetcar propelled electrically from an overhead wire, that follows a set of tracks.

Tuberculosis: An infectious disease that can affect the lungs, caused by an organism. Also called "TB" for short.

Zonta Club: History Club

INDEX

Allen Canyon – 39-41, 49

America Theater – 95, 101

Amethyst – 39

Animal – 1

Anaconda – 125

Antelope – 11

Anticline – 1

Archaeological – XV, 1, 199

Archery Range – XIII, 105, 114-117, 119

Arminto – 203

Air Force – 2, 33, 38, 174

ARC – 155

Army – 33-37, 99-100, 163

Arrows – 115-117

Artifacts – 199, 207

Asbell Ranch – 195

Asbestos – XIII, 43, 66, 123, 125
    Mine – 89-98, 145
    Road – XIV, 135
    Spring – XV, 56, 66, 89-90
    Wyoming Asbestos Co. – 39

Aspen Lane – 144

Astoria – XIV, 213-215

ATV – 85

B-24's – 113

Bates Hole – 191

Bear – 1

Bear Trap – XIII, 127, 144-145, 147, 158-165, 167, 169

Bessemer – 194, 216

Bessemer Bend – 194, 214

Bighorns – 113

Bi-Rite – 203

Black Hills – XIV, 35

Blackmore Ranch – 32

Bloody Turnip – XV, 30, 39, 47

Bobcat – 1

Bomb Shelter – XV, 167

Bootleggers – 199, 212

Braille Trail – 104, 147

Bridle Trail – 48, 55-64, 67

Brookside Inn – XV, 66, 85-86

Brooks Lake – XV, 21
    Ranch – 9, 21

Buffalo – 213

Bullwinkle's – 203

Bumps a Daisy – 145

Camp Dodge – XIV, 33

Cancer – 91

Carey Act – XIV, 27

INDEX

Casper College – 203
    Country Club – 69
    Creek – 33, 35
    Fire Department – 40
    Lions Club – 147
    Mountain cave – XIII, 167-168
    Mountain Road – XV, 66-68, 73-77

Cattle Depression – XIV-XV

Cave – XIII, 83, 167-168, 208

Cavern – 167-168

Cemetery – 33, 38, 75, 111

Center Street – 95

Circle Drive – 51

Chair Lift – 134-140

Chinook Wind – 2

Choppers – XV, 19-20

Chromium Mine – 127

Civilian Conservation Corps (CCC) – 36, 55, 144, 155

City of Casper – 135

City Park Loop – 147

Clear Fork of Muddy Creek – 17, 21

Clovis Point – 1

Coal Mountain – 1, 113, 194, 217

Coast to Coast – 203

Columbine Circle (Sunshine) – 144

Columbine Drive – 144

Continental Divide – 213

Copper – 119-123

Copperopolis – XVI, 119-122

Counterfeiter – 199

Country General – 203

Courthouse – XIV, 94-95

Coyote – 1

Cowboy State Games – 149, 155

Crimson Dawn – XIII, 99, 144, 157, 169, 171-184,

Cronin Ranch – 243

Cross Country Ski – XIII, XIV, 85, 99, 148, 147-150

Crystal Canyon Garden – 13

Crystal Cave – XIII

CY – XIV, 10, 27
    Canyon – 27, 31, 47

Dance Floor – 99

Dry Creek – 33, 34-35

Deadwood SD – 125

Dean's Sporting Goods – 203

Deer – 1, 31, 48, 60

Deer Creek – 9, 21, 30

Deer Haven Park – 144

Dempsey Stables – 66-67

Department of the Interior – 147

INDEX

Dixie Lodge – 66, 145

Dubois – 21

Dugway – 67

Eadsville – XIII, XIV, 13, 39, 47, 105, 113, 124-133, 149, 167

Eagle – 157

Earthquakes – XIV-XV, 1

East End Road – XIII, 171-172, 173

Elk – 1

Elkhorn Canyon – XIII, 69-71, 157
    Creek – 69, 126, 147
    Fire – 70
    Hermit – 69
    Springs Campground – 144

Elk Mountain – 113

Elks Lodge – 145

El Rancho No Dinoro – 144, 188

Equestrian Path – 67

Falls – 11, 50-54, 135

Fallout Shelter – 167

Feldspar – 126-127

Ferris Mountains – 113

Fire – XIV, XVII, 1, 27, 63, 109, 145, 167

Fish Hatchery – XIII, XV, 9, 11-12, 213-214

Flood – 51

Fort Bragg – 20

Fort Caspar – XIV, 10, 34-38, 55

Fort Fetterman – 36

Fort Russell – 33

Fort Washakie – 111

Four Wheel Drive – 171, 189

Fox – 1, 199-201

Fredericks' Cabin – XIV, 191

Freeland – 191

Freezout Hills – 113

Fremont Canyon – 213

Fur Trading – 213

Galena – 125

Galena Queen – 69, 126

Garden Creek – XIV, 31, 69, 146
    Falls – XIII, 17, 27, 30, 33, 48, 49, 50-54, 73, 79, 83
    Road – 31-32, 48, 49, 51

Geology – 1

Gering Nebraska – 213

Ghost Town Fire Fighters – XVI-XVII

Girl Scouts – XV, 111-112

Glades – 17

Gold – 13, 125

Goose Creek – 126

Goose Egg Ranch – XIII, XIV, 27, 194, 207, 214, 216

INDEX

Gallery – 209
    Restaurant – 207, 209

Gothberg Canyon – 212
    Ranch – 32

Gothmore Park – 32

Governor – XIV-XV, 21, 24, 27

Granite Mountain – 113

Gravity Hill – 30, 49

Green Houses – 13-14

Green Mountain – 113

Guinard Bridge – XIV, 34

Hairpin Turn – 66, 73-75

Hahn Sawmill – 17

Hang-Glider – 79

Hat Six Creek – 126
    Falls – 9, 11
    Hogback – 9, 11
    Ranch – 9, 171
    Road – 9, 11, 19, 171, 189

Hayden Expedition – XIV, 207, 210

Hellfighters – XV, 204-205

Hells Half Acre – XV, 205

Henning Hotel – 95

Hermit – 69

Hidden Treasure Mine – 39, 127

Hiking – 64, 69, 135

Hiking Trails – 55-64, 83

Highway 220 – 187, 195, 199, 203-207, 217

Hiland – 203

Hogadon – XIII, XV, 43, 67, 103, 105, 111, 113, 115, 125, 134-140, 149

Hogadone Trail – 27, 30, 31, 47, 135

Hogadone Tram Trail – 56, 61-62, 97

Hogback – 11

Hole in the Wall Grotto – 167

Hotels – 95

Ice Canyon – 168
    Cave – 168

Independence Rock – 34, 213

Indians – 1, 10, 21, 33-38, 51, 112, 213

Information Sign – 104

Inn Bar – 243

Jackson Canyon – XIII, 194, 207-212

Jaycee – 90

Jenkins Trench – 190

Junction – 143-144

Killkare – 85

Kortes Dam – 243

K2 Tower – 105, 149

Lady Lancers – 39

Laramie Mountain Range – 1

Lathrop Cabin – 70, 73-74

INDEX

Lathrop Turn – 66, 73

Layman's Corner – 74

Lead – 125

Lewis & Clark Expedition – XIV, 111-112

Lion – 1

Lions Camp – XIII, 127, 144, 154-155

Lions of Wyoming – 155

Livestock – 2

Look Out Point – XIII, 66, 78-81, 83

Lumber Camp – 16-18

Maps – X-XI, XIII, 30, 66, 83, 105, 134, 144, 148, 158, 194

Maud – 39

Micro Road – 100, 113, 115

Midsummer's Eve – 173-186

Miller Sawmill – 16-18

Mills Spring Camp – 104, 157, 169

Mills, WY – 159

Mine – XIV, 13, 70-71, 89, 107, 119-133, 168

Miner – 145

Montana – 125

Moonshine Lode – 107, 109

Montgomery Hill – 67

Morad Park – 34

Mormon Ferry – XIV

Mosteller Ranch – 11-15

Mountain Bike – 83, 99, 153

Mountain Lion – 1

Mountain Top Baptist Assembly – 104-105

Mountaineer's Mercantile – XIII, 39, 66-67, 99-102, 149

Muddy Creek – 9, 17, 21

Muddy Mountain – 1, 21, 104, 113, 142, 149, 159, 169, 187-190, 213

Museum – 173-178

Mystery Mine – 116

Mythology – 173

National Guard – 99-100, 163

National Recreational Trail System – 147

Natural Bridge – 156-157

Natrona County Parks Board – 115

Natrona County Road Bridge & Parks Dept. – 159

Needle Eye – 72

Nordic Skiing – XV, 144, 149

Norse – 173

North Casper – 94

North 40 Ski Trail – 157

INDEX

North Platte River – XIII, XIV, 33, 36, 205, 207, 213, 215

Nuclear Attack – 167

Nursery Ski Course – XIII, 144, 145

Oil – 24

Oil Mountain – 113

Oregon Trail – XIV, 34, 213

Outer Drive – XIII

Overland Trail – 213

Paint Rock – 70

Parks – 160

Parks Dept. – 149, 174

Paleo – Indian – 1

Patee Road – XIV, 31, 44-45

Pathfinder Dam – 94

Pearl Harbor – XV, 145

Pedro Mountains – 113

Pegmatite – 125

Phanwaeist – 39

Pitchpin – 171

Picnic – 51, 159

Picture Frame Rock – 157

Pine Mountain – 113

Platte Bridge Station – XIV, 33-38, 51

Platte River Fly Shop – 194, 203

Pomma Lift – 135-136

Ponderosa Park – 104, 169, 171

Pony Express – XIV

Poplar – 31

Poison Spider Creek – 214

Poison Springs Creek – 214

Post Office – 191

Powder House – 166

Pratt Ranch – 69

Price Dairy – 195

Railroad – 2, 21, 27, 191

Ranch(ing/er) – XIV, 2, 21, 27

Rattlesnake Mountain – 113

Red Butte – XIV, 34-38, 173-174, 184, 194, 204-205

Red Creek – 17

Red Rocks – 83

Red Springs – 214

Reservation – 10

Reshaw Bridge – XIV, 36-38

Rock Climbing – XIII, 66, 82-84

Rock Chuck – 55

Rotary Club – 51

Sacajawea – XIII, XIV, 105, 111-112

Sage Grouse – 1

INDEX

Saint Anthony's Church – 40

Salting – 89

Saw Mill – XIII, 16-18

Scandinavian – 145

Schooner – XIV, 21

School – 13, 17, 203

Shady Nook – 1

Sheep Wagon Hill – 104, 169

Shirley Mountains – 113

Silver – 123, 125

Skiing – IX, XIV-XV, 85, 105, 134-140, 144-146, 148-150

Skunk Hollow – 144, 147

Slash pile – 151, 169

Slaughter House – 199

Smith Creek – 9

Snowboarding – 135, 139

Snowmobile – 85, 104, 144, 158-159

Snowshoeing – 85

South Dakota – 1251

South Pass – 213

Spanish Folklore – 173

Speas Fish Hatchery – 213-214

Spillway – 145

Split Rock – 59, 83

Spring – 89, 125

Star Wallow – 144

Stewart Camp – 155

Street Car – XIII, 105, 106

Still – 100

Strube Loop – 144, 147, 149

Summer Festival – 162-163, 165

Sunrise Shopping Center – 83

Suits Me – 107-110

Sweetwater River – 213
    Station – 34

Switch-backs – 135, 171

"T" Bar – 135

Telegraph – XIV, 33, 35, 145

Telephone – XIV

Tennessee Walkers – 194, 202

Thunder Bolt Ski Course – 66, 145-146

Timberline Sporting Goods – 203

Tipi Canyon – 171

Torrington, Wyoming – 213

Tow rope – 135, 145

Tower – 113, 149, 169-170

Tower Hill – XIII, 169-170, 173

Townsend Hotel – 95

Transcontinental Railroad – XIV

INDEX

Tuberculosis Camp – 124, 133

Turkey – 1

Ugly Bug Fly Shop – 203

Upper Limestone – 83

U.S. Department of the Interior – 147

V-V – XIV, 10, 21-24

WA-WA Lodge – XV, 99-102, 129

Wells Fargo – 39

Werner Wildlife Museum – 195

West Fork of Muddy Creek – 11

Whisky Peak – 113

Whitaker Cabin – 31

Wild Oats Lane – 93

Window Rock – XIII, 74, 156-157, 190

Witches – 173-184

Wolcott – 66

Wolf Creek – 194, 195-197

Wolton – 203

Wolves – 1

Woodland Theater – 180

World Chief Guide – 111

World War I – 155

World War II – 55, 105, 113, 127, 145, 155, 185

Wylan Turn – 66, 73

WYOBA – 144, 155

Wyoming Blvd. – 66, 195

Yellowstone – 210

PEOPLE INDEX

Adair, Red – 205

Adams, Robert L.(Bob) – 115-117, 168, 208

Ahrndt, JoAnne – 181, 183

Allen, Bess Opal – 107

Allen, "Happy Jack" John D. – 39-41, 123

Allison, Ryan – 153

Amacher, Desirae – 154

Amacher, Fred – 154

Anderson, MAJ – 34

Antram, Jesse E. – 35

Arbiter, Frank – 51

Arnold, John – 70-71

Asbell, Bill – 78, 195-197

Asbell, Sue – 195-197

Astor, John Jacob – 213

Baden-Powell, Lady Olave – 111

Bailey, A. C. – 39

Ball, Ken – 99-100

Ballau (Bellew), James – 35

Baptiste – 111

Basil – 111

Bessemer, Sir Henry   216

Bower, Pat – 153

Bonwell, W.T. – 33-35

Bourbon, Kent & Anna Marie – 53

Bowron, Paul – 180

Bretney, CPT – 34-35

Briden, Mr. – 17

Brooks, Abby – XIV, 21

Brooks, Bryant B – XIV, XV, 9, 21-26

Brown, Dave – 153

Brown, Moses – 35

Brown, William – 35

Burgess, Austin – 153

Burgess, Don – 135, 146

Burke, Micky – 243

Burrow, F.H. – 123

Butler, G. E. – 210

Butler, Tom – 153

Buxton, Marshall – XV

Cabot, Bruce – 205

Camp, George – 35

Carlson, Dick – 162

Carey, Joseph M. – XIV-XV, 27, 216

Carey, (Robert D.) – 94

Carrigen, Eleanor – 11, 174, 177-178

Carrigen, Tom – 75, 101

Chadderon, Dave – 153

PEOPLE INDEX

Charbonneau – 112

Clark children – 132

Coates, Fred – 195, 199

Collins, Caspar – XIV, 33-36

Collins, William O. – 34-35

Colter, John – XIV

Cook, Cal – 127, 130

Cook, Mrs. Cal – 130

Cook, Wil – 121

Cotherman, Phyllis – 181, 182

Crazy Horse – 37

Cridor, Jim – 15

Crockett, David B. (Davy) – IX, XV, 43, 107-110, 168

Cronin, Barney – 145, 243

Cronin, Corey – 161, 168

Cronin, Joe – 2

Crooks, Robert – 213

Culp, Adam – 35

Cummings, Jack J.R. – 101-102

Cummings, Tom – 165

Currier, S.A. (Jack) – XIV, 123, 125

Curry, Peggy Simson – 70

Custard, Amos – XIV, 33-38

Day, John – 213

Daine, J.E. – 210

Determan, Darlene – 31, 39

Diesburg, Mike – 153

Dodge, G. M. – 33-35

Doherty, James – 83

Downey, Kerry – 181, 183

Durst, Dyann – 181, 182

Dye, Kevin – 64

Eads, Charles W. – 91, 123, 125-126

Edgerly, Len – 31, 39

Elliot, H.W. – 210

Erbert, Ray – 19

Farrell, Claire – 149

Forsling daughters/children (Ogilbee) – 11, 174

Forsling, Jim – XV, 99, 173, 180, 185

Forsling, Neal – XV, 11, 99, 157, 173-185

Fougstedt, Nils – 99-100

Fougstedt, Oly – IX, 99-100, 129

Fredericks, John & Zelta – 191

Freeland, Bill – 191

Furlong, Dave – 135

Galles, Don – 199-201

Galles, George – 201

Galles, Gladys – 201

PEOPLE INDEX

Galles, Walt – 199, 201

Garner, J.L. – 123

Garton, Maude – 17

Gates, Justin – 163

Glasgow, Susan – 181, 183

Gothberg, Ed – 214

Gothberg, Martin J. – 214

Gray, William D. – 35

Green, Martin – 35

Guinard, Louis – 34

Hall, Charlie – 162

Hamilton, Rice B. – 35

Hanson, Paul – 162

Hardesty, Bob – 106

Harrison boy & girl – 51

Harrison, Dwight – 49

Harrison, Samuel – 51

Harshman, Pat – XVI

Hayden Dr. F.V. – 210

Heil, George – 35

Hemry, Kathleen – 2

Henry, Don – 181, 182

Hiney, Shorty – 121

Hobbs, Bill – 39

Hogadone, Charles C. – XIV, 31, 91, 123, 135

Hoover, Kathy – 111

Hoover, Mildred – 111

Hoover, Peggy – 111

Hopkins, Ruth Joy – 97

Hoppe, August – 35

Horton, John – 35

Houston, Harold – 199

Houston, John – 205

Houston, Walt – 199

Huffard, Gladys – 191

Hunt, Rebecca Weaver – 179

Hunt, Travis – 153

Iams, E.E. – 51

Icenogle, Chris – XVI

Ilgner, Arno U. – 83

Irwin, John – 121, 127

Jackson, William H. – 207-212

Jacques, Doris – 201

Jacques, Paul – 199, 201

Jenkins, Carl – 190

Jennings, Bill – 154

Jones, Ben – 213

Katie – 179

PEOPLE INDEX

Keating, Father James – 40

Kerns, Ed – 51

Kicho – 151

Kressner, Hope – 162

Layman, Brenda – 75

Layman, Fred – 74-75

LeClerc, Francis – 213

Leeper. J.F. Dr. – XV, 69

Lenhart, Dave – 199

Lewis & Clark – XIV, 111-112

Lisco, Dick – 167

Littlefield, Clarence – IX, 85

Littlefield, Pearl – IX, 85

Long, William B. – 35

Loomis, Jean – 174, 185

Lund, Steve – XV, 1, 199

Magoon, West – 75

Mahoney, Tim – 2

Martin, Alex – 180

Martin, Dave – 180

Martin, Mary – 178-179

Martz, Rick – 153

Mathews, Marge – 201

Mattern, Dane – 120

McClellan, Robert – 213

McCune, Lee – 147

McDonald, George W. – 35

McGrath, "Post Hole" Jack – 22

McManus, Don – 146

Meckling, Dean – 107

Merritt, Mr. – 126

Messers – 123

Miles, Vera – 205

Miller, Dusty – XV

Miller, "Sawmill" – 16-17

Miller, William H. – 35

Miner, Lee – 145

Miner, Pete – 154-155

Minium, A. E. – 13, 91

Montgomery, Matt – 67, 91, 123

Moonlight, Thomas – 33

Moore, Kelly – 82-83

Morris, Esther Hobart – XIV

Morrison, Chuck – 214

Mosteller, Charles – 11-15

Mosteller, "Pistol Billy" William – IX, 11-15

Motten, Woody – 153

Myers, George – 121, 127

PEOPLE INDEX

Nehring, Sebestian – 35

Nelson, Abe – 123

Newby, Mr. – 51

Newby, Mrs.& child – 51

Nicolaysen, Mary Hester – 111

Nicolaysen, P.C. – 111

Okie, F.W. – 13

Olson, Dave – 70

O'Quinn – 89

Osborne, Dwight – 146

Patee, Fred – 43-46, 91,107, 137

Paxton, Elizabeth – 181

Pennington, Bob – 201

Perkins, Dick – 146

Perry, Don – 106

Peterson, Clayton – 106

Plumb, COL Preston B. – 33

Powell, Thomas – 35

Price, Mary – 195

Pursel, Whitey – 202

Randall, Art – 56, 70, 89, 119

Red Cloud – 37

Reed, Bernadine – 86-87, 131

Rhodes, Rufus – 10

Robertson, Bill – 168

Robertson, Rob – 145-146

Robinder, Rob – 203

Robinson, Peter – 153

Rodolph, Aaron – 153

Romanek, Jack – 215

Roosevelt, Franklin D. – 55, 95

Ross, Katherine – 205

Ross, Nellie Tayloe – XV

Roszel, Marty – 153

Rude, Dustin – 153

Sacajawea – XV, 111-112, 127

Sahlnecker, PVT – 33

Santistevan, Phil – XVI

Schafer, Ferdinand – 35

Schramm, Kelly – 153

Scott, John – 181-182

Searight, Mr. – 214, 216

Seely, Fred – 51

Shakespeare – 176

Shrader, Corp – 35

Simpson, Arthur Mrs. – 128

Simpson, Floyd – 128

Simpson, Frank – 128

PEOPLE INDEX

Smith, J.B. – 39, 123

Smith, James – 51

Smith, Nellie – 40

Spears, Mark – 153

Speas, Dan – 214

Sproul, Samuel – 35

Stewart, Allen H. – 155

Strube, Ed – 147

Stuart, Robert – XV, 213-215

Stuckenhoff, "Doc" – 21

Summers, Edwin – 35

Swanton, Tom – 153

Sweeney, Brandon – 153

Troutman, Glen – 165

Truman, Bess – 181

Truman, Harry – 181

Turnbull, Dr. C. S. – 210

Tull, Samuel – 35

Uptain, Seth – 153

Vallar, Andri – 213

Van Burgh, Dana – 147

Wales, Matt – 154

Wallace, Bess – 181

Wayne, John – 204-205

Weakland, Debbie – 181

Weaver, Chris – 180

Weaver, Warren – 109, 146, 185

Weaver, Wayne – 146, 185

Weis, Norman D. – 214

West, William – 35

Whitaker, Ray – 31, 195

White, 1SG Samuel B. – 33

Wister, Owen – 207

Wolf, Matt – 153

Wright, Frank Lloyd – 75

Young, Brigham – XV

Young, Thomas – 35

Zahn, Henry – 123

Zerby, Dave – 19-20

Zinn, Jacob – 35

Zinn, John R. – 35

Zook, Andrew – 153

ACKNOWLEDGMENTS

ADVERTISEMENT

Wa-Wa Lodge – Wenger collection

MAPS

Glenn Bochmann
Geological Survey
Arno U. Ilgner
Natrona County Roads, Bridges & Parks Dept.
Dorothy Putnam
Wyoming State Parks and Historic Sites

PHOTOGRAPHY

AERIAL: Dana Van Burgh, with Pilots Judy Logue and Linda Wackwitz

HISTORICAL: Ken Ball, Tom Carrigen, Tom Carrigen; Wyoming Division of Cultural Resources, Tom Carrigen courtesy the Weaver Collection, Elly Carrigen, Bob Dorn Courtesy the Asbell Collection, Don Galles, Charlie Mosteller, Audry Cook McGraugh; courtesy Bernadine Reed, Chuck Morrison Collection; courtesy of the Casper College Library, Natrona County Pioneer Museum, O'Quinn, Dorothy Putam, Art Randall; courtesy Casper College Library, Rob Robertson, Frances Seely Webb Collection; courtesy Casper College Library, Norman D. Weis and the Wenger Collection.

RECENT: Kevin Anderson, Dave Ball, Bob Bondurant, Kim Wrasper Cronin, Vaughn Cronin, Bruce Nichols, Pierre Nichols, The Kelly Moore Collection, and Darin Walker.

GENERAL HELP

Kevin Anderson at the Casper College Library, Natrona County Library, Eva Babcock, Carma Ball, Bob Bondurant, Robyn Broumley, everyone at B&B Pharmacy, B.F. Cronin, Jim Doherty at Back Country Mountain Works, Lisa Edmondson at the Casper Star-Tribune, Rick Ewig and John Hank at the American Heritage Center, Kelly Estes at the Natrona County Parks-Road & Bridge, Anne Heberline, BLM, Parks Department, Hollie McHenry and Cindy Brown at the State Archives Office in Cheyenne, WY, Shirley Jacob at Casper College, Mary Lou Morrison at The Book Gallery, Susan Niethammer True, Zula Safford, Ed Strube, Shelly Trumbull, Dana Van Burgh, Gary Vantrese at Hogadon, Rick Young at Fort Caspar, The Writing Center at Casper College, the family for their patience, and of course everyone on the Interview and Bibliography pages.

Photo of the author at Jackson Canyon by Robyn Hamilton.

ABOUT THE AUTHOR

Vaughn Stephen Cronin is a Wyoming native, born in Casper in 1955. He graduated from Natrona County High School in 1974, and later received two associate degrees from Casper College. Vaughn is the unit administrator and Battalion Legal NCO for the Wyoming Army National Guard in Casper. Vaughn has also been known as a local musician, real estate salesman, and former board member of the Brooks Water & Sewer District. Vaughn's father was employed for many years as a civil engineer for the U.S. Bureau of Reclamation. He worked on construction of Kortes Dam, later moving back to Casper to work on projects over a three state area.

His grandfather William S. Cronin, came from Cork County Ireland, to the U.S. in 1895. He first came to Wyoming in 1901. He established the Cronin Sheep Company north of Casper, and in the Bighorn Mountains, in 1905. The company was disbanded after Mr. Cronin's death in 1946. He also owned the Home Hotel and the Inn Bar, and now the site of Stas's Restaurant. His nephew Micky Burke owned the building with a furniture store next door. W.S. Cronin was also active in oil, and stocks.

Other Books by Vaughn Stephen Cronin.

Learn to Drum
By
VAUGHN CRONIN

LEARN TO DRUM
Booklet and Cassette

HOW TO ORDER BOOKS

from

VAUGHN'S PUBLISHING

Mail Check or Money Order to:

VAUGHN'S PUBLISHING

P.O. BOX 4181
CASPER, WY 82604

vaughnspublishing.com

BOOK TITLE: _____

YOUR ADDRESS:

NAME: _____

MAIL ADDRESS: _____

CITY: _____

STATE: _____ ZIP: _____

NUMBER OF BOOKS: _____

COST PER BOOK {$16.95}: _____

ADD $3.20 SHIPPING PER BOOK: _____

TOTAL: _____